AF567121

DREAMTIME
MOON

ABORIGINAL MYTHS OF THE MOON

DREAMTIME
MOON

ABORIGINAL MYTHS OF THE MOON

Charles E. Hulley *with paintings and drawings by* **Ainslie Roberts**

First published in 1996 by
REED BOOKS
a part of Reed Books Australia
Level 9, North Tower
1–5 Railway Street
Chatswood NSW 2067

Text copyright © 1996 Charles E. Hulley
Illustrations copyright © 1996 Ainslie Roberts Pty Ltd

ART AUSTRALIA

All rights reserved. No part of this publication may be reproduced, stored in a retrieval system or transmitted in any form or by any means, electronic, mechanical, photocopying, recording or otherwise, without the prior written permission of the publishers.

National Library of Australia
Cataloguing-in-Publication Data:

Hulley, Charles E.
Dreamtime moon: Aboriginal myths of the moon.
Bibliography.
ISBN 0 7301 0491 5.
1. Aborigines, Australian - Legends.
2. Aborigines, Australian - Folklore.
3. Moon - Mythology. 4. Moon - Folklore.
I. Roberts, Ainslie, 1911 - 1993. II. Title.

398.26

Set in 12 1/2 Perpetua by Reed Books
Printed in Hong Kong by South China Printing

For Eva, Christopher, Michelle, and all who cherish the living power of the moon

The myths on which so much of Aboriginal culture is based are a precious part of the Australian heritage, and in acknowledging the subtle makers of the tradition to which the public myths used here belong, I must also recognise those who, over the years, have collected and helped to preserve this treasure of archetypal material.

To my knowledge, *Dreamtime Moon* is the first subject-specific book of Aboriginal myths, save for a few specialist studies of the Rainbow Serpent. It is a book for the general reader. Its main aims are to recount a representative selection of Aboriginal myths about the Moon, to examine the fascinating themes they contain, to comment on parallels from other cultures, and to encourage readers to discover, or rediscover, the wonder of the living landscape that surrounds them.

The book is illustrated by a selection from the Dreamtime paintings of my friend, the late Ainslie Roberts, AM, who has done so much to stimulate popular awareness of Aboriginal culture and whose work is a constant source of inspiration to me.

I am grateful also to Phillip Adams for allowing me to quote from his thoughtful account of a meeting by moonlight, *Stopping for Death on a Moonlit Evening*.

As you open these pages I would like you to imagine a place you love by moonlight. Perhaps it is a garden, or a beach, or a view of the sea—but wherever it is, if you look closely there will be a special quality about the light that brings the wonder of childhood to life again and peoples the shadows with phantoms of an earlier time, when our ancestors sat around the campfire after a day's hunting, and old, wise men and women told stories of creatures that haunt the dark and the night sky, and how the world became as it is.

Much of the time we act as if nature is only a resource to exploit, but there is a paradox here, for it is not like that in the private world of our dreams and imagination. There nature is not dehumanised, inanimate, dead. There we thrill to the sight and sound of birds and animals in the wild. And there we seek out quiet places charged with a special atmosphere, which we might call numinous or sacred, and for which the Aborigines have their own word, *djang*.

Men and women of our secular time often need help to bring the landscape they encounter to life and to focus their feelings about it. This is true worldwide, but in Australia the Aboriginal myths that have been preserved are an aid and heritage beyond price. Some are children's stories or are told that way; some are efforts to explain the natural world of the hunter-gatherer; but others are creations of great power and move us (even those of us who stand outside the tradition) in the same way as music and poetry, more a matter of instinct than reason, more a matter of moonlight than the harsh light of day.

In this collection of Aboriginal myths about the Moon I include two in which there is a female Moon—one from Tasmania, the other from the mouth of the Murray River in South Australia—but the overwhelming majority tell of a male Moon and a female Sun. This may appear strange at first, but it is true of many early societies where the change to the grazing of animals and agriculture had not yet taken place—for, as we shall see, it was mainly with the organised tending of crops that the nurturing Moon became a feminine deity, while the Sun seems to have become male and dominant with the rise of patriarchal kings and the growth of conquest, trade and city-states.

For Aborigines, the Moon brought two profound gifts: fertility and the hope of life after death. The Moon was a fertilising male, who conferred the power to reproduce on women, as well as on plants and animals. From Australia and New Guinea to Alaska, the Moon was husband to all women, and if a girl feared getting pregnant she took care not to catch the attention of the Moon-Man or look at him too closely. The Moon governs the waters in which its reflection floats. It produces floods and controls the tides. Its twenty-eight-day cycle is nature's clock. With its three dark days and pattern of growth and decline, it is the master of death and rebirth; and its bright and dark aspects link it with opposites such as good and evil, male and female, being and non-being.[1]

The appeal of the Moon's beauty and strange enchantment is as strong today as it was during the last Ice Age, when its symbols were already being carved and revered.

Not long ago writer and broadcaster Phillip Adams wrote an article that he called *Stopping for Death on a Moonlit Evening*.[2]

It is one o'clock at night, and he is driving from Sydney to his farm. 'Coming over the hill,' he says, 'I see the Moon loom hugely before me, as yellow as a caution light and acne'd with craters.' Ahead, two hitch-hikers, a boy and a girl, stand by the road, flinching slightly from the wind of the night-time trucks that roar by. As Adams slows to pick them up, he thinks 'they look unreal, as if the headlights are projecting them'. It is late, and already we have entered the phantom world of the Moon and its juggling with the mind.

The young couple is heading for Newcastle, but Adams will be turning off at Cessnock and cannot take them all the way.

Now the Moon is off to the right. It has lost its 'atmospheric magnificence' and is just an ordinary Moon again. The girl says: 'My dad died today.' And somehow that association of Moon and death moves the imagination. 'It was sudden,' she says, 'an accident. He was forty-eight.' It makes her listener think of his own daughters. Her father's death evokes mine, he writes.

The names of the young people are Kylie and Jason, but they are not just phantoms of the night—they are a real boy and girl experiencing death for the first time—and, as one does with strangers, they talk about their lives until the road forks and Adams has to let them off.

'I'm sorry,' he says, grieving suddenly for all the death in the world. And as the figures of Jason and Kylie vanish behind him, the Moon reappears. 'It has lost its golden glow. It is now as small and white as ... Kylie's face in the back seat—trying to comprehend for the first time in her life what death is all about.'

This is not just a casual encounter of the road. We are hearing a tale from the edge of the camp fire, of how the Moon governs death, and journeys, and perhaps the renewal of life.

The Bones of the Moon

Many Aboriginal myths describe how death came to the world and the Moon escaped the fate that binds the rest of us. Coastal tribes are particularly concerned with death and rebirth, and the three myths on this theme that follow come from the shores of Arnhem Land.

The first tells how Alinda the Moon-Man and Dirima the parrotfish were two quarrelsome companions, who constantly bickered over matters of no importance. This often led to physical violence, and during one disagreement they wounded each other so badly that both of them died. The spirit of Alinda became the Moon, and Dirima entered the sea as the parrotfish. But in that Dreamtime world, death was not final and this did not satisfy Alinda, who chose to continue his old quarrel. 'When the parrotfish or anyone else dies,' he said, 'they can never return to life.' He spoke without thinking, for he was trapped by his own rash decree. He had to think quickly while choice was still valid, and rather than share the common fate he elected to die for three days each month and then return for another brief cycle of life.

In the second myth, which establishes death and rebirth as facts without relating them specifically to humankind, the story comes from a series of songs called *The Moonbone Cycle*.[3]

Singing sticks are beaten, wooden trumpets are blown, and the women dance in the moonlight while they sing how Moon lived with his sister, the Dugong, in the plains bordering Arnhem Bay. Their home was the Claypan of Moonlight, which became a billabong when it rained. Dugong collected lily bulbs and lotus roots for them to eat, but she was constantly bitten by leeches, and one day she stormed home crying in irritation: 'I've had enough of these leeches, brother. I'm giving up land life to enter the sea and become a dugong.'

'What shall I do?' asked Moon.

'You can stay in the sky,' said his sister, 'but first you must die.'

Moon considered this. 'I won't die like other people though,' he said. 'I'll always return to life again.'

'Do as you like,' said Dugong, 'but not me. When I die I won't come back, and you can pick up my bones.'

'I'm different,' her brother told her, 'When I die, I'm coming back. Each time I grow sick I'll become very thin and follow you down to the sea, By then, only my bones will be left, so I'll throw them away and die.' Become pure spirit, he meant, 'But after three days I'll rise again and return to the sky.'

'What about your bones?' Dugong asked the question because the bones of the dead are impregnated with life-force, and their fate is an important Aboriginal concern.

'You'll find them on the beaches,' said Moon, 'and meanwhile I'll grow new ones.'

The Claypan of Moonlight became a Dreaming centre. Moon left his spiritual reflection in the pool it contains, and his bones became the shells of the chambered nautilus.

The idea of nautilus shells as the skeletons of dead moons is a lovely touch of imagination. They are washed up on the beaches of the area by tides, which also have a relationship to the Moon. When the tides are high, water runs into the Moon and fills it. As the water runs out, the tides decline, and for three

Birth of the New Moon

dark days the Moon lies empty. Then the sea rises once more and slowly fills it again.

In the third myth, two Dreamtime beings shaped like men arrive from Goulburn Island, off the northern coast of Arnhem Land. One is Djabu, which means a small spotted bush cat; the other is Moon. As they travel together they shape the landscape and give each place a name. At Cooper's Creek they catch fish and fill their baskets with goose eggs. Further south they pull out their whiskers one by one and plant them by the water to become bamboo. At last they find a good camping site and live there until sickness sweeps through the land. In spite of their power and the burning of magical sweet-scented leaves, they can't combat it. 'If we die,' they tell each other, 'no one will ever come alive again,'

Djabu dies first, but Moon is a clever man, a Man of High Degree. He survives and begins using enchantment to revive his friend, but he cannot succeed. Perversely, or bound by some inner law, Djabu will not cooperate; and without the help of the patient, Moon cannot restore him to life. At last Moon gives up. 'Very well,' he says, 'Djabu's body will die forever; only his spirit will stay alive. But it is different for me. I will keep on coming up with a new body.'

'Now,' say the people of the area, 'the law is that when we die they just bury us. Our spirits stay alive, but our bodies can't come back—and it's all because of that Djabu!'[4]

The Tiwi people of Melville Island tell a more humanised story. For them, the first man in the world was Purukupali. He had a wife named Bima, and a small son, Jinini, to whom he was devoted. Each morning Bima went off to collect food, taking Jinini with her and bringing him back at the end of the day. But during these trips she formed a liaison with Japara, one of the unattached men of the tribe, and as their passion for each other increased she began to neglect her son and leave him more and more alone. One hot day she stayed in the bush with Japara even longer than usual; when she returned, the shade of the tree under which she left Jinini had moved, and he was dead of exposure to the heat. Distraught with grief she chanted a song of remorse: '*Bili wangia tingatia*—Evil woman am I to have caused the death of my son.'

Purukupali was so angry he beat the unfaithful Bima almost to death and hunted her into the bush, where she became the curlew that wanders through the trees at night calling for her lost son.

'As my son has died,' cried Purukupali, 'so shall the whole of creation die, and once dead they will never come to life again.' Japara argued with him and pleaded for Jinini's dead body: 'If you will only let me have it,' he said, I'll restore him to life in three days.' But Purukupali was adamant. All his rage at Bima's infidelity smouldered beneath the surface, and soon the two men were locked in a deadly struggle. They were both wounded and worn out from the fight, but refusing all help from his enemy, Purukupali picked up his son's body and backed into the sea, chanting his eternal curse: 'You must all follow me. As I die, die must you all.'

As the waters closed over Purukupali's head, Japara rose into the sky and became the Moon. But he was not quick enough to escape Purukupali's curse.

Bima, the Frightened Curlew

He too must die for three days each month. The scars on his face may still be seen on the disc of the full Moon, and the place where Purukupali died is marked by a great whirlpool in Dundas Strait, between Melville Island and the mainland.

When Japara is reborn after his monthly death, he feasts on mangrove crabs, consuming them in such quantities that by the end of two weeks he sickens and dies—never learning, doomed to repeat the same pattern forever. The silver crescent of the new Moon is his skeleton, and the shadow of the old Moon cradled within it is Imunka, his dark spirit.

A kinder version of the myth tells how Purukupali and Japara were friends, who discovered how to make fire by rubbing two sticks together, or perhaps by seeing lightning strike a dead tree. Like Prometheus, Purukupali taught his discovery to humankind so they would have light and warmth and a means of cooking food. To make the gift a true part of nature, he gave a large torch of bark to his sister Wuriupranili, who became the Sun-Woman, and a smaller one to Japara, who became the Moon-Man.

At first Japara returned to the east by way of a path that ran beneath the southern horizon, but he stumbled on a hornets' nest. The angry insects stung his face so badly it remains scarred to this day, and having learned his lesson he now uses the same underground passage to the east as Wuriupranili.

So we can choose our explanation for the 'acne' marks on the face of the Moon: Purukupali's club, or the hornets that Japara disturbed on his unlucky journey to the east.

☾ ☾ ☾

In Aboriginal Australia the creation of the world that we know took place in the Dreamtime, a 'fabulous' epoch when supernatural beings, who until that time had slept beneath the surface of the earth, rose to create the world we know.

The stories of the Dreamtime are the foundation of all social and religious life. They recount the journeys of these primordial beings and show how the landscape was shaped, how fire was created, how plants, animals and humans were made, and even how necessities such as spears and grinding stones were invented to help Aboriginal men and women with their daily lives.

The Aranda, an inland people, say that in the beginning the earth was like a desolate plain. There were no hills or rivers, and no light either, for the Sun, the Moon and the stars still slumbered under the earth. Nor were there any plants or animals, only semi-embryonic masses of half-developed infants lying helplessly in places that would later become salt lakes and water holes.

These shapeless infants could not develop into individual men and women, but neither did they grow old and die. Indeed neither life nor death as we know them were present on the face of the earth. But beneath the surface, life did exist in the form of innumerable supernatural beings, who slumbered there awaiting a call to emerge. What summoned them to awake we do not know, but one day their eyes opened and they broke through the surface to impregnate the land with their energy and power. The Sun and Moon rose too, and the earth was flooded with light. It is a remarkably complex cosmogony, or theory of creation. To create humankind, these beings, 'born of their own eternity',[5] used stone knives, first to release the arms and legs of the *Inapatua*, as the embryonic infants were called, then with four swift cuts to make fingers and toes. Eyes and mouths were opened, noses and ears were moulded, and the previously shapeless *Inapatua* grew swiftly to adult size.

Some of the Creators took the form of birds and animals, others that of completely formed men and women. But in most of them, human and animal were linked. Those who looked like animals acted like humans; those who looked like humans could shift their shape to become the particular animals with which they were associated. In this regard we should not think of an animal form as inferior to a human one. For millennia animal forms were the highest expression of sacred power. That is why the Stone Age hunters of Europe, who depended on animals for survival, decorated their cave walls with vibrant paintings of deer, and bison, and mammoths, both to ensure an increase of the species and to honour the most potent images of life they knew. In their totemic life, therefore, Aboriginal men and women, like the Creators, combine both human and animal characteristics, and in Dreamtime myths they change freely from one to the other.

In *Aranda Traditions*, T.G.H. Strehlow gives a glowing description of what the Burt Plain, bordering the northern ridge of the MacDonnell Ranges (northwest of Alice Springs), was like in the Dreamtime. Each creek and rill contained water. The plain was green with herbs and grass. The mountain slopes were covered with wildflowers. The air was heavy with the scent of eucalyptus and acacia buds. Native bees hummed in the pale yellow blossom of the bloodwood trees, eager to collect nectar—honey being a great delicacy, which Aboriginal people call 'sugarbag'. There was an abundance of game: wallabies in the hillside caves, sharp-nosed bandicoots in the burrows, eagles

Numbakulla and the Inapatua

that swooped from the clear skies and, when dusk fell, euros that would hop down the slopes to graze. It was then that the Sun covered her face with hair-string ornaments, and the Moon strode out of the mountains like a proud young man. He wore a chaplet of gleaming white bandicoot tails and stood on the edge of the plain admiring his bright face mirrored in the water.

It is the Garden of Eden without the Fall, because although no one, not even the old wise men, can say why the Dreamtime came to end, before it did rituals were established to ensure that its energies were not lost. At a certain moment the Creators became a part of the landscape where they had been active. Where they lay, life-force was concentrated, and if the ancient rituals were invoked in the right way, the past became present once more and the participants, provided they had been properly trained and initiated, could enter the Dreamtime, one with their ancestors and the transforming power of that early world.

☾ ☾ ☾

Aboriginal myths are generally silent on moral issues.[6] They avoid spelling out the rights and wrongs of a situation or condemning actions as weak and vicious. In myths, as in life, there are often acts of treachery, theft, greed, lust and antagonism. Violence is never far beneath the surface of mythic life, and little provocation is needed for it to erupt.[7] The same is true of the gods and heroes of the Greeks, and the knights of Arthur's Round Table. But there, just as the stories are more familiar to us, the motivation and social background are more familiar too.

For example, why should Purukupali refuse the help of Japara to resurrect his son and march off into the sea? Jealousy and the refusal to accept help from the enemy would be factors, but the myth may also tell us that, even in the Dreamtime, men could act against their own best interests and that Purukupali was caught up in a vast web of cosmic necessity, forcing him to establish things as they are. Alternately, phenomena so difficult to understand may have an inscrutable causation too.

Because of its regular cycle, the Moon measures and unifies.[8] The patterns it imposes are the patterns of all nature and suggest an ordered society of rules that must be obeyed even when they lead to events as terrible as those in *Ngilindi and the Net of Death*, a myth associated with several locations, including Dildula near Mulangimbi, and Dultulla, an island in Buckingham Bay, northeastern Arnhem Land.

Ngilindi the Moon-Man had two wives. They were sisters, and each bore a son. Every day the women went searching for food, but as Ngilindi grew older he preferred to stay in camp and allow his young sons to do the hunting.

One day they speared a whistler duck. When Ngilindi saw what they had, he bustled about and made a fire. The boys cooked the duck, but they ate it themselves and gave none to their father. This was a great transgression, for it is an obligation of the young to provide food for their elders. Ngilindi protested, but the boys said they had been hungry after their efforts, and anyway they were off hunting again and would find him something else.

Ngilindi, who had been sitting with his back to them, shrugged and continued to weave a fishing net out of grass. The net is called a *tarkul* and is like a long bag.

When the boys returned with a goose they had speared, their father once more made a fire, and once again his sons cooked the bird and ate most of it themselves. 'Here is a leg,' said the eldest at last, tossing the food to him in an offhand way.

Now Ngilindi rose and picked up his net. 'I'm going fishing,' he said, 'but first I want to see how the net holds. Go inside, my sons, and test it for me.'

Dull with all the food they had eaten, the boys crawled into the net. At once Ngilindi closed the throat and tied the end with a strong rope. Now the boys began to be frightened. They struggled and screamed for their mothers, but the women were too far away to hear, and Ngilindi slung the bundle over his shoulder and strode out into the lagoon. When he reached deep water, silently, without another word to the terrified boys inside the net, he flung it away and watched it sink. Then he walked back to the camp.

At dusk the women returned and asked where their sons were. 'They have gone a long way,' said Ngilindi, looking into the failing light. 'But where?' asked his wives. Ngilindi shook his head. 'I don't know,' he said.

Suspicious, the women left him some yams and went out to search for tracks that might provide a clue to the whereabouts of the boys. The elder followed Ngilindi's footprints to the lagoon, and there beyond the reeds that grew along the shore she saw a shadow floating in the water. Calling her sister she waded towards it and in horror found herself looking down at the dead faces of the two boys.

Cutting the bodies free, the women filled the night with their cries of grief, but it was too late to revive their sons. All they could do was carry the bodies back to camp and bury them.

There was no doubt who was responsible for the deed, and Ngilindi did not try to conceal what he had done. A law of family and tribal life had been broken, and the culprits had paid for it with their lives. At the same time neither Ngilindi nor his wives wanted to stay in the camp where the bodies were buried, and so the little party moved on.

When they found a suitable place for a new camp, the wives said: 'You build a humpy for us to sleep in, Ngilindi. We'll find something to eat.'

The humpy, with a hole in the roof to let out the smoke, was finished when the women returned with a good supply of food. They were seething with resentment, but they gave no sign of it as they fed their husband and settled down with him for the night.

A fire burned in the centre of the floor, The old man was asleep, and at midnight the two sisters crept out into the darkness. They blocked the doors and closed the smoke hole. When that was done, they set the humpy alight. 'Your life for the lives of our sons,' they shouted in triumph as Ngilindi choked with smoke and shook the branches of the flaming walls.

Soon his cries ceased. The fire crackled and roared through the night until the humpy collapsed in a shower of sparks. Ngilindi's charred body lay sprawled among the embers, but as the fascinated women watched, it began to writhe and move. They clasped each other in terror as the shape of the dead man grew thin and began to glow with a cold light. Slowly it became a chilly crescent, then it grew full and round and floated into the branches of a huge *gurreri* tree, to rest among the white blossoms.

'*Wiribigili*,' whispered the voice of their dead husband, a word that carries the sense of: 'Father, forgive them for they know not what they do.' And more strongly: '*Wiribigili*. Now all husbands will die like me, and all wives will die like you. You burned me alive because I killed your sons. Very well, when your time comes to die, you will die altogether. I am different, I have died, but, as you see, I am alive again.'

At first he slept there, regaining power. Then he drifted from tree to tree, ascending through the branches until he reached the sky and became the Moon.

This is a powerful myth of broken taboos and bitter revenge. The images are compelling: the old man silently weaving his net of death, the screams of the terrified boys, the grief of the women bearing their drowned sons in their arms. Then the blazing death hut; the ghastly moment when the corpse of Ngilindi begins to shudder and change; and the whispering voice in the moon-lit night pronouncing a doom of death on the world. These Dreamtime events from the early days of creation were not just tales of long ago, they were a part of everyday life, although their full impact was reserved for special occasions and moments of personal significance.

☾ ☾ ☾

The sacred Moon Tree is a very ancient image. It was especially common in Assyrian and Babylonian pictures, where it gradually evolved from a flourishing tree covered with fruit to a phallic stump or pillar. This recalls some of the earliest representations of the Moon deity in which Mother and Moon Goddesses such as Astarte and Cybele were worshipped in the form of white cones and pyramids, or even more simply as black meteoric stones—connecting the erotic nature of Moon deities with both male and female elements.[9]

The Moon Tree finds an echo in many Australian Aboriginal myths in which a tall tree or a magically rising tree forms a ladder for the Moon-Man to reach the sky at a critical moment in his story. The myth of *Wira the Moon* is one of these. This version comes from the Flinders Ranges in South Australia, although there are many others.[10]

Wira the Moon-Man was the bad-tempered elderly uncle of two youths, whom he was obliged to instruct in their tribal duties. Although Wira was a good teacher and trained the boys thoroughly in magic and hunting, he seemed lazy and self-indulgent and soon began to leave most of the work to them.

A crisis arose when they came running into camp to say that they had found an emu drinking at the creek. 'Stay here, uncle, and we'll spear it and bring it to you,' they promised excitedly. But Wira forbade it. 'No spearing,' he said. 'Bring a net and stretch it across the creek. Then I'll tell you what to do next.'

Wira was a hard taskmaster and criticised his nephews unmercifully as they struggled to arrange the heavy net as a trap. When this was done at last, he told them to frighten the bird in the direction of the net and let him know when it became entangled. This they did, again offering to spear the bird and bring it to him. Once more their uncle forbade it. 'Young men must not touch emu meat,' he said, 'and certainly may not eat it.' This was a part of their training in learning obedience and the tribal custom of providing food for their elders—as in the case of Ngilindi and his two sons—and perhaps because the emu is sacred to the Moon and they were dealing directly with the Moon-Man. Wira walked down to the creek, slaughtered the bird himself and then made a fire to cook it, while the youths who had done all the work of catching it stood by, shifting from foot to foot with irritation.

To make them feel better, Wira said: 'The other day when I was out by myself I noticed a tree full of witchetty grubs. Come along and I'll get some for you.'

He took them to a tall tree and, good to his word, he climbed up and began to throw down juicy grubs for them to eat. But the boys had put up with

Wira Reborn

enough of what they considered his tyrannical ways. Once he was high in the branches they used a spell he had taught them to make the tree grow. Urging him to climb further, they watched in triumph as he reached the top and exclaimed in surprise to find the sky so close. Before he knew what was happening, the young men set the tree shrinking again and left their uncle stranded in the sky. 'That's your punishment,' they mocked. 'You'll stay up there now, except for three days a month when you'll descend to a valley in the mountains. There you'll die, and when you're reborn you'll rise again to the sky. That is your fate. And so it will be forever!'

Now Wira was truly the Moon, his power increased, and his mortal nature fell away. Thinking they were free, the two youths ran off to enjoy their feast of forbidden meat. It was not to be, for as they ran, Wira drew them into the sky and turned them into two stars, under his control forever.

From the fruit of the Moon Tree comes *soma*, the drink of immortality, inspiration and secret knowledge. The crown of the Moon Tree rises to heaven and the roots extend to the underworld, where Sinn, the Babylonian Moon God, and Osiris, the Egyptian God of the Underworld, judge the dead in their three dark days.

A variation of the *soma* theme is an Aboriginal myth which tells that in the Dreamtime people did not die, because each month the Moon gave them a magic drink that restored them to life. The villain here was the bronze-winged pigeon, who opposed this magic with his own. He had the cumulative power of vast flocks, for the bronze-wing existed in enormous numbers until its habitat

Birthplace of the Moons

was destroyed, and from then on only the Moon could overcome death. A myth collected by Spenser and Gillen during their nine weeks' stay at Tennant Creek in Central Australia during 1901 suggests that *soma* is really the blood of the Moon.

One day, the Moon—a Warramungu man from the north, in this incarnation—camped by a water hole at the foot of the Murchison Ranges. He saw there the tracks of a woman but did not find her until early the next morning. Soon he had charmed her into sitting down with him and launched into the rapid intimacy that is common in encounters with the Moon. Deeply engaged, they failed to notice two eaglehawk men who had recently discovered the use of fire and, unable to manage it, had inconveniently ignited a large tract of the surrounding country.

'Look,' cried the woman, sitting up in alarm as she felt a breath of heat from the flames, 'there's a big fire over there, and it's coming our way.'

'Never mind,' murmured the preoccupied Moon, drawing her down again, 'it's still a long way off.'

But she had been right. When they looked again it was too late, and a wall of flame surged over them. Moon, who was a supernatural being, remained unharmed, but the woman was so badly burned that she died. At once Moon opened a vein and sprinkled her with his blood. The magic fluid restored her to life, and when she opened here eyes, not only were her terrible burns healed but she was as young and beautiful as she had been before the accident.

At this point our curiosity is engaged; we wonder what adventures the restored woman and lascivious Moon will have next. Was she given a divine nature by her brush with death and treatment with the magical blood of the Moon? Are there to be further transformations and more lovemaking? We do not know. All we are told is that they went up into the sky together, and the myth ends.

Sometimes the Moon Tree grows in a grove or garden. It makes a charming appearance in the Aboriginal myth of *The Birthplace of the Moons*. This tells of a valley where the soil is the richest on earth. There grow the huge Moon Plants, which bear Moons instead of fruit. When a Moon is mature, it breaks from the parent plant and drifts through the valley until it is time to enter the night sky. The Sun nurtures the plants and helps the Moons to grow, but once they invade its domain it pursues them across the sky in a jealous rage, consuming them piece by piece until nothing is left but a mist of gleaming fragments that become stars.

Certain animals have always been associated with the Moon. The crab is one of these. Its eye-stalks retract, and it can disappear into its shell; some species hide in the mud, others live in tidal pools, a pattern of withdrawal and reappearance, which reminds traditional people of the Moon. Mangrove crabs were the favourite food of Alinda the Moon-Man,

The Rebirth of Japara

and in Western astrology the sign of Cancer (the Crab) is governed by the Moon.

The frog, as will be seen, is also a moon creature—as are bears, which hibernate in winter, and animals whose horns resemble the curve of the crescent Moon. Australia has no horned animals, but a reminder of the new Moon is found in the curve of the boomerang and the shape of certain beaches, which become Moon sites. Predictably there is a Kowanyama children's tale in which the new Moon is a boomerang caught in the sky.

Snakes have a lunar character as creatures of fear and mystery that live in dark places, bear their young in eggs, and share the Moon's gift of renewal by shedding their skin. Snakes are connected with sex and fertility, and share that phallic role with the Moon too. In a number of Ophite jewels, Cybele, the orgiastic Phrygean Goddess from what is now a part of Turkey, offers a goblet, probably containing *soma*, to a snake. The symbol of Cybele was the crescent Moon, often shown in union with the Sun,[11] while the Ophites were a Jewish Gnostic sect, also from Phrygia, who revered the serpent as a symbol of hidden, divine wisdom, and flourished in early Christian times[12]—the combined images from two different religions, reinforcing the transcultural connection between the serpent and the Moon.

Snakes are also the hunting companions of Bahloo, an important Australian Moon deity, who helped create girl babies. In some places the bite of the serpent was thought responsible for a girl's first menstruation, and of course the 'period' generally occurs in a 28-day cycle, like that of the Moon. The Maori of New Zealand called menstruation *mata marama*, Moon sickness, and believed a girl's first period to be caused by the Moon seducing her while she slept. In India and the Torres Strait Islands one word is used for both Moon and menstrual blood.

In Australia the possum and, to a lesser extent, the emu are the principal Moon animals. In the case of the emu, the connection is obscure. However, being sensitive to correspondences in nature, the Aborigines would know that the female emu lays her eggs and then leaves them for the male to incubate; that makes the bird a male creature with moonlike eggs and the role of nurturing new life.

The reasons for connecting the possum with the Moon are more obvious: it is a night animal, it climbs tall trees, it is easier to see when a full Moon is shining, and its eyes gleam in the dark like small moons.

One of the great Dreamtime hunters was the possum man Moodai. He had two sons, whom he liked to take on hunting trips, and at night as they sat by

The Search for Moodai

the fire he would point to the clear, inland sky and fascinate them with tales about the Moon. One night when they were hunting, Moodai climbed a tall thin tree, so high it seemed to disappear into the sky. He threw down a good meal of witchetty grubs and, telling the boys to hold the tree steady, climbed on until he reached the top. 'I can touch the Moon,' he shouted, exciting them so much they let go the tree and jumped back to see what their father was doing. The tree was too slender to carry the weight of the man without being held. It began to sway and bend, there were shouts of alarm, and as it came crashing down, Moodai sprang to the Moon for safety. He has lived in the Moon ever since. The boys climbed all the tall trees in the area, but none was high enough to bring the Moon within reach. They became albino possums with moon-coloured fur, and the whole tribe of possums still climb trees in a never-ending search for the great hunter.

☾ ☾ ☾

A striking Moon and possum myth that I call *The Moon and the Sun-Woman* comes from the vicinity of Balgo, a remote town in the Great Sandy Desert.

Although Wadi Yalgan the Moon-Man was a hunter of possums, he killed only small animals, storing them in his long, thick hair. He always hunted by night, and on one occasion, returning to his camp in the small hours of the morning, he discovered two strangers waiting for him. They had found no water, for Wadi Yalgan kept his supply carefully hidden, but guests were entitled to hospitality, so he shared moon water with them and then went off to collect wood for a fire. The strangers had been surprised to see no meat

Sun-Woman and Moon-Man

in the camp either, but when their host returned he took a possum from his hair and tossed it on the flames. At first it was only a small creature, but Wadi Yalgan commenced a strange chant as it cooked, and the possum increased in size until it was large enough to feed all three of them. After his guests had eaten, Wadi Yalgan warned them to hurry home before morning and avoid the nearby camp of the Sun-Women or run the risk of being burned to death.

The strangers left well before dawn, but they did not listen to the Moon-Man's advice and called at the camp of the Sun-Women on their way. Most of the women were sleeping, but two were awake, and as they were very beautiful, with golden bodies and flaming hair, the men worked hard to charm them. At last the women agreed to leave their sisters, and the foursome walked on until they found a good place to camp. But Wadi Yalgan knew what he was talking about, and the moment the men reached out to touch the women, they were consumed in a flare of radiant heat.

Wadi Yalgan soon sensed that something was wrong. He had gone out hunting and found no possums, which told him that nature was out of harmony. He guessed the problem involved the strangers, and picking up his axe and a water carrier he followed the tracks of the men and their companions until he found two charred bodies and two sets of female footprints leading back in the direction of the Sun-Women's camp. Guessing what had happened, and blaming the women for trying to make love to mortals, he decided to teach them a lesson. It was daytime now, and finding the Sun-Women dancing wildly in the shimmering heat, he attacked them with his axe. But although in his fury he cut off arms and legs at random, the severed limbs just whirled through the air and rejoined the bodies from which they had been hacked, while the Sun-Women danced wildly on as if nothing had happened.

Because the daytime vitality of the women was too strong for him, the Moon-Man returned to where he had left the bodies of his visitors and laid them in a sacred rock pool. At first nothing happened, but when he returned from another possum hunt he found that the vitalising water of the moonlit pool had restored the men to life. 'Go straight home,' he told them, 'or you will be killed again and this time I won't help you.' They had seen enough, and fled without another word. Nature was in balance again; the Sun-Women went on dancing by day and sleeping by night; and the Moon-Man hunted his possums at night and slept in the shade of his camp during the day.

The myth confirms the belief that the Moon controls the waters of immortality. He is a magician who knows the secrets of life and death, and the possum is his sacred animal. Under the name Japara, he offered to restore Jinini to life after three dark days; and here he does successfully restore men who have been scorched to death in the fiery female realm of the Sun. Thus to all people the ever-returning Moon offers hope that death may not be the end after all.

☾ ☾ ☾

To the native tribes of Central Australia, the name of the Moon-Man is Atinya. He was a possum man who died and was reborn as a boy. When people saw him rise from his grave, still covered in earth, they were frightened and ran away, but Atinya pursued them calling: 'Don't be afraid. Do not run away from me, or you will die forever. I have died once and I will die again, but then I will rise a second time and you will see me in the sky.' He had already assumed his divine nature and quickly grew to adult size. The prediction once made became a fact. Atinya did die a second time and reappeared in the sky as the Moon. Since then he dies each month and is reborn, say the Aranda, but the men and women who fled from him die forever.

Another Central Australian myth tells how a possum man carried the Moon about with him on a shield. During the day he hid it in a cleft in the rocks, but one night an Unchurka man of the seed totem (who would also need fertility and growth from the Moon) saw a light glowing on the ground. This proved to be the Moon lying on the possum man's shield, where he had left it while he climbed a tree. The Unchurka man seized the shield with the Moon on it and fled as fast as he could. Furiously the possum man gave chase, but failing to catch the thief, he stopped and shouted: 'You may not keep the Moon. It will go up into the sky and light everyone at night.' As he spoke, the Moon rose from the shield and sped into the night sky, where it has remained ever since.

The famous collection of myths and fairy tales assembled by Jakob and Wilhelm Grimm at the beginning of the nineteenth century, in what is now Germany, has only one concerning the Moon. However, the atmosphere has so much in common with the Australian myths examined here that it is worth including for comparison. Called simply *The Moon*, it tells that in days gone by there was a land where the nights were always dark, the Moon never rose, and no star shone in the sky.

Four young wanderers set out from this country and arrived in another kingdom. There, when the sun set behind the mountains, they saw a shining globe, which hung in an oak tree and bathed the landscape in soft white light.

The young men asked a countryman who was driving by in his cart what sort of light this was. 'That's the Moon,' he replied. 'Our mayor bought it for three talers and fastened it in that oak tree. He has to pour oil on it each day and keep it clean so that it will always burn clearly, and for that service he receives a taler a week.'

When the countryman was gone, one of the young men said: 'We have an oak tree as big as this at home. Let us take this Moon with us, and the nights won't be so dark.'

'I tell you what,' said the second, 'Let's fetch a horse and cart to carry it.'

'I'm a good climber,' said the third, 'I'll bring it down.'

When the fourth, who had nothing to add, had found a horse and cart, they carried out the plan, and in their dim homeland everyone greeted them as heroes who would make life more comfortable than it had ever been before.

The four took care of the Moon for many years and received a taler a week for doing so. But finally they grew old, and when one became ill he instructed that a quarter of the Moon should be cut off and laid in his grave, since that quarter was his property. When he died, the mayor climbed up with a pair of hedge-shears and snipped off a quarter of the Moon to be placed in the coffin as instructed.

So it was with the other three. When each of them died, another quarter was buried, and with the death of the fourth the nights were as dark as they had been before.

But that wasn't the end of the matter. The pieces of the Moon passed beneath the earth and into the world of death, where they were reunited. The bright light soon roused the dead from their sleep; they sat up very pleased with the change and resumed their former way of life—some attended dances and the theatre, others rushed off to the inns—and before long there was so much uproar that the noise was heard as far off as Heaven.

St Peter, who guards the gate to Paradise, thought there was a revolt in the lower world and hurried down with an army of angels to quell it. But when he found out what had happened, he simply told the dead to lie down in their graves again, took the Moon away from them and hung it in the sky, where it remains to this day.[13]

Many familiar elements are present in this story: the four young men who represent the phases of the Moon, the tree, the association with death and revival, the insistence that the cosmic law of death be enforced, and the final removal of the Moon from earth to the sky. The superficial trappings may be different, but with a few changes of costume, geography and custom, the Grimm Brothers' tale could be easily retold as part of the Aboriginal tradition.

Stories like *The Moon* are marked by what Padraic Colum in his Introduction to *The Complete Grimm's Fairy Tales* calls 'the rhythm of night'. The stove and the hearth has replaced the camp fire, and the freedom of the hunter-gatherer has shrunk to a village world where the mayor could be expected to take charge of a valuable asset like the Moon. If a piece had to be cut off, the mayor would climb the oak tree where it hung and perform the operation with his hedge shears. In medicine the wise woman was as important as the doctor, and the waxing and waning Moon would determine the time of month when herbs used in preparing her remedies had to be picked. But the power of the Moon did not stop with its influence over simples: in Wales, for example, the Moon had power over warts, and snails and frogs were used in their cure. The Welsh would take a snail with a black shell (to invoke the magic of the dark phase of the Moon) and pin it to the branch of a tree using as many thorns as there were warts to remove. When the snail decayed, the warts were said to disappear. If a frog, an important Moon creature, was used, it would be impaled on a stick and rubbed on the warts. When the luckless creature died, the warts were supposed to vanish. Sir James Frazer, who reports these cures in *The Golden Bough,* does not say whether they worked.

☾ ☾ ☾

As far back as the last Ice Age the phases of the Moon and their magical qualities were well known. Traditional people lived so close to the edge of survival that they had to be intensely aware of practical connections in the natural world on which they depended. The Moon was 'the heavenly body concerned, above all others, with fertility and the rhythms of life', a constant companion in the night sky that showed time 'in a concrete sense'. In the Siberian cultures of the Ice Age, for example, we already find the symbolism of spirals, snakes and lightning connected with the Moon as a 'measure of rhythmic change' in nature,[14] while the shell with its erotic shape, the Tree of Life, and the Nurturing Mother, have all been associated with the Moon for thousands of years.

Many Aboriginal myths offer glimpses of a distant past inhabited by giant animals, lit by volcanoes, now extinct, and subject to climates very different from those we know today. This is true of two Tasmanian myths collected by Jackson Cotton,[15] and told to him by Timler, whom Cotton describes as High Priest of the Brayleny, the religious hierarchy of the island. These open a window on a period when the island was cold enough for icebergs to be observed near the coast sufficiently often to demand an explanation when they ceased to be seen.

In the Dreamtime, Tasmania (or Trowenna, to give it the Aboriginal name) was a small sand-bank in the southern sea. Night shrouded the world until Parnuen the Sun, and his wife, Vena the Moon, rose from a frosty sea adrift with floating ice and brought light where there had been none before. As they passed over the island on their daily journey, they dropped shellfish around its shore and seeds of the great gum tree, *tara monadro*, on the sand, which they

The Birth of Trowenna (Tasmania)

sprinkled with rain. We are told this was done by the Sun, or the Sun and the Moon together, but the Moon has always been associated with dew and rain, and it was probably Vena who did it. She would certainly have scattered the shellfish in the sea around the island, for, in the case of a feminine Moon, shellfish, because of their vulvalike shape, belong to her.

Trees sprouted, leaves fell and mixed with the sand to become earth, and as the shellfish died and became rocks and mountains, the present shape of Trowenna rose from the sea.

Vena could not travel as fast as Parnuen, and he carried her in his arms. However, when he grew tired he would leave her on one of the icebergs, picking her up on his way back from the west. There seemed no risk in this, but one day the iceberg on which Vena reclined melted, and she sank

The Melting Moon

Rhys Roberts

in the depths of the sea. Enraged by the loss of his wife, Parnuen melted the icebergs with solar fire and gave the island to their son, Moinee, the Great South Star. But that did not restore Vena, and although she rose from the sea after three days, they never again travelled the sky in each others' arms.

This is the only version of the myth we possess, but it is likely that the Moon played a larger role in the mythic creation of Tasmania than Timler's patriarchal account allows.

Another account of a female Moon comes from the sweep of coastline where the Murray River meets the Great Southern Ocean. Here the myth

Death of the Moon-Woman

describes a female Moon as well as a female Sun and is based on her deeply erotic nature. 'It seems', writes the prim Dr Wyatt, JP, who reported the story in 1879, 'that the moon is a female of very light character, associating freely with men' and 'not particularly chaste'.[16]

The waxing Moon was attributed to the greed of a Moon-Woman who fed on roots so nourishing she quickly grew fat. Her sexual appetite waxed too, and at the peak of her cycle she joined the tribesmen each night for an orgy so intense that she wasted to a skeleton. In that unattractive state she was driven away (perhaps to the land of the dead, which the Sun-Woman passed each day) and did not return until she wanted more men.

The sympathetic magic of the Moon is still strong in the modern world: I know a woman who associates *Death of the Moon-Woman*, the Ainslie Roberts painting inspired by this myth, directly with the recommencement of her own period after a gap of nine years.

We have seen what an important part the Moon played in the creation of Tasmania, where the rocks and mountains were formed from shellfish dropped by Vena and her husband, the Sun. The Roman historian Pliny also associated shellfish with the Moon. Their numbers increase, he believed, with the waxing of the Moon, whose lunar energy penetrates everything.

The Moon imposes a pattern on all nature. It is therefore not surprising to find in a myth of the South Australian Dieyerie tribe that all creatures were made by Pirra the Moon under the direction of a creation spirit named Mooramoora. As the first men and women moved about the land with moonlight alone to guide them, it was bitterly cold and dark, and they could not see to hunt the giant emus and smaller creatures they needed for food. Desperate for a better life, they prayed to Mooramoora, and the creation of the Sun was his response. The ceremonies reenacting the event are dismissed as too obscene to describe[17]—further confirming the role of the Moon. Rites of a orgiastic sort are typical of lunar mysteries, as we have seen from the behaviour of the Moon-Woman of the Murray Mouth.

With the creation of the Sun, the Dieyerie tribe believed that night had to be established once more. This was done by a vast flight of bats that covered the sky with their wings at sunset and did not return to their caves until dawn.

The flight of the Bats

☾ ☾ ☾

The Moon weaves a vast web of being, in which nothing stands alone. It matters little whether we are dealing with the adoration of the Moon itself, a person inhabiting the Moon, or a lunar personification. Natural objects, be they mountains, trees, Sun, Moon or stars, are worshipped not for their own sake but because they reveal some ultimate and interconnected reality.[18]

As it was in the Dreamtime, so it is now. The Aborigines inhabit a humanised realm. The countryside is their 'age-old family tree'.[19] The most dismal landscape is charged with awe, and all individuals, women and men, are affiliated to a dreaming spot where they can make contact with their origins and renew their sense of meaning. They believe with a profound conviction that they were physically present when the events described in the myths took place—the doings of their totemic ancestors were their own, and each of them played a personal role in that glorious adventure before time as we know it began, which they do not so much learn about as remember.

Of course, Australian Aborigines are not alone in their sensitivity to the powers and properties of nature, represented in this account by the Moon. When an African Masai saw a new Moon he threw a stick or stone at it and shouted: 'Give me strength' or 'Give me a long life'.

In earlier times, Estonians thought the misfortunes of the month could be shifted from their own shoulders by greeting the new Moon with the words: 'Good morrow, new Moon. I must grow young as you grow old. My eyes must grow bright as yours grow dark. I must grow as light as a bird as you grow as heavy as iron.'

The crescent Moon is a charm for increasing flocks and herds. Women throughout Western Asia once wore it to bring them more children, and some women in southern Italy still wear it as an amulet to secure ease in childbirth.[20]

It follows that the Moon also increases money. *Turn your money in your pocket whenever you see a new Moon*, goes the song. But the full ritual is to look at the Moon over your left shoulder (left being the side of instinct and the unconscious), bow or curtsy (depending on your sex), take out your money, turn it over, and walk on without looking back.

It is wise to settle everything that has to do with increase during the waxing Moon: sheep should be shorn to ensure the rapid regrowth of their wool; fields should be readied in the Moon's first quarter for seed to be sown, else it will rot in the ground. Even today some French farmers sow at new Moon, and prune and pick their vegetables when the Moon is on the wane so as not to oppose the rhythm of nature.

Trees should be felled at the wane of the Moon. At the end of the nineteenth century, bills for the sale for timber in France still contained an assurance that the wood had been cut at the waning Moon. And as late as 1928 Cuban law forbade the felling of timber for railway sleepers during the Moon's increase.

Spartans, the most famous warriors of the Greek world, would march to war only when the Moon was full. This stopped them sending troops to oppose the Persians at Marathon and almost changed the history of Greece *and* Europe. Even Roman Emperors were not above seeking aid from the Moon. Tiberius, who was balding and worried about it, would not allow the sparse hair that was left on his head to be cut before the new Moon had appeared.

From the observation that dew falls more thickly on cloudless nights, the Moon came to be associated with gentler forms of moisture (as we have seen in the myth of the creation of Tasmania) as well as with tides, floods and menstruation.

A simple Moon myth from the Awabakai tribe explains how the Belmont Lagoon, near Newcastle, New South Wales, was formed. Once Belmont (*Bah-Tah-Bah*) was all bush, and above it shone Yellana the Moon, whose sacred spirit was Pontoe-boong the Moon-Man. He was a great traveller and often journeyed so far that people of earth could see only a small part of him. One night, brooding on the beauty of Punnal the Sun-Woman, he began to weep with frustration. Soon the tears of the Moon collected in a pool, which swiftly became a lagoon. Onlookers gathered to watch the streams of silver light that were forming a lake where none had existed before, and as he wept, Pontoe-boong drew closer to the earth, flooding the landscape with moonlight. I will

The Night the Moon Cried

make sure that this lake never dries up, he thought, then people will always see my reflection and admire it. The Belmont Lagoon became sacred to the Moon-Man, and tribes gathered there to celebrate his rites. Not long ago a plaque designed by Ainslie Roberts was placed on the site to record the myth.

The disasters of flood and storm are also gifts of the Moon—at once the destroyer of outworn forms, and master of the growth and regeneration that follows.

Our most famous flood myth, the Biblical tale of Noah and his ark, has many lunar elements. *Noah* is probably a version of Nuah, the name of a Babylonian Moon-Goddess; the dove he released to see how far the waters had gone down is frequently associated with Moon deities; and even the word *ark* has linguistic affinities with *argha*, the Hindu word for crescent, and *arc*, meaning the segment of a circle—making Noah's vessel a Moon boat.[21]

The Moon has both nurturing and destructive aspects where rain is concerned. In the Classical world the Moon-Goddess, under many names, sent spring rains to nourish the young crops—but there were also special rites for persuading her not to let the rain fall too heavily in August, when it could ruin the harvest. In Greece, August 13 was the great festival of the Moon-Goddess Hecate, and later, in Rome, of her counterpart, Diana. These goddesses were entreated to prevent summer storms, and in Christian times August 15 was chosen as the feast of the Assumption of the Blessed Virgin, who, like the pagan goddesses before her, was invoked to prevent storms until the harvest was in.

An Aboriginal myth concerning the Kendi or rain-dragons can be related to the Moon, although there is no direct reference to it. Lizards often appear in Moon myths, while the Kendi possess a moonlike frill and are mythologically associated with thunder, lightning and rain.

At a time when Central Australia was still a fertile part of the continent, creatures bred so rapidly that there was not enough food and shelter for them. Long discussions as to what should be done took place, but no agreement could be reached; and the Kendi, who were powerful magicians, finally lost patience. Retreating into the hills they called up a vast storm. The flood that followed submerged the whole area, and when the waters subsided the few creatures that escaped enjoyed a more secure life.

Another deluge myth concerns the frog, an important lunar animal in many countries. Tiddalik, the largest frog ever known, awoke one morning with what Charles Mountford calls 'an unquestionable thirst'.[22] He commenced drinking and drank so much that there was no more water left in the whole

The Rain Dragon

world. The land began to dry up, the trees shed their leaves, and it was clear that if action was not taken soon, the animals would begin dying too. A council was called and searched in vain for a way out, until a wise old wombat suggested that if Tiddalik could be made to laugh the water would flow from his mouth and they would be saved. Creature after creature tried to amuse the giant frog, but he just blinked his eyes and ignored them. Finally, the eel (or

Tiddalik the Frog

perhaps a snake) began to dance. The shapes he twisted himself into were so comical that Tiddalik shook with laughter. Out gushed the water from his mouth, and flowed off to replenish the earth.

In many countries people see the shape of a frog in the Moon. The frog's amphibious habits relate it to both water and land and therefore to the opposites that the Moon reconciles. Like the Moon, frogs vanish and reappear—with the rains, in their case—giving them a lunar nature and linking them with death and rebirth. In Egypt thousands of small frogs would appear a few days before the Nile overflowed and were seen as heralds of the fertility it brought. Frog-gods were placed on Egyptian mummies, and the goddess Heket, who had the frog as one of her attributes, assisted Isis in the ritual resurrection of her husband Osiris, both of whom were associated with the Moon.

As well as holding centre stage in the deluge myth of Tiddalik, called onomatopoetically *Dak* by the Kurnai tribe, frogs play an important role in a myth I will call *The Eye of the Bunyip*. This was told to C.M. Peck[23] in the 1920s by a young Aboriginal man who was camped with two women on a reserve near Burryja Station in New South Wales. On the night Peck heard this tale, the Moon had not yet risen, the women had crept out of sight, and the young man kept glancing apprehensively over this shoulder as if the act of narration would evoke the dangers of which it told.

'Before the Murray River was formed by the great hunter Nurrunderi,' he began, 'it was only a large billabong surrounded by trees, and bushes, and reeds.' There, at dusk one night, came a Bunyip, which sat on the bank opposite an Aboriginal camp. He was grey-brown in colour and blended into the night, a shadow among the trees. There too came a young hunter stalking ducks. When he had speared two fat ones, he waded back through the reeds and prepared to return to the camp.

At this moment the Bunyip, which must have been a manlike creature, reached out to seize him, but the hunter slid back into the water and swam softly to a safer place.

His heart was pounding as he scrambled back to land, and ran towards the fires of the camp, shouting a warning of what had happened. In a moment the camp was in an uproar. Indeed, the only person not impressed was the girl the hunter was to marry. In spite of his warning to stay back, she came gaily to meet him, poking fun at his fears and trying to calm him down. The approach was fatal. The Bunyip seized her and carried her off to his lair in a nearby swamp.

At this point Peck remarks: 'I'll pass over the detail ... of what happened in the camp and how they called to each other and ran back and forth in alarm...' (an example of how easy it is to rob a narrative of its impact and reduce it to the level of a tale for children).

All night long the young hunter listened in despair to the screams and struggles that came from the swamp, but at night the powers of evil dominate, and neither he nor anyone else could help her.

At first light he hurried towards the swamp. Tracks confirmed that this was the direction the Bunyip and the girl had taken, and as he followed them he made a plan. Catching some frogs, he tied their legs together, fastened them to a stake and drove it into the soft earth at the swamp's edge. There he waited in hiding until dusk, but the Bunyip did not appear, and as the light failed the hunter was forced to give up and return to camp. The threat of darkness was very real to him; his whole training told him that his plan could not succeed until the sun shone again.

Next morning the frogs were gone. Patiently, day after day, the hunter repeated the ploy—capturing frogs, binding their legs and staking them out—but the Bunyip would not be lured into the open by day.

Soon it was time for the tribe to move on. They urged the hunter to give up, but he refused, and they left him stubbornly waiting for the Bunyip to appear by daylight and give him a chance to rescue the girl he loved.

The day after the tribe departed, rain began to fall. The morning was so heavy and wet that the Bunyip, thinking it was dark enough to be safe, emerged from the swamp with the girl behind him and walked towards the frogs.

With a shout the young hunter leapt from his hiding-place. The Bunyip roared defiance. The girl held out her arms and wept, but she was entranced by the Bunyip's magic and could not run to her lover's side.

The eyes of the opponents locked. The hunter threw a spear and missed. The Bunyip hurled one of the frogs, and, hitting his enemy in the face, blinded him in one eye. This meant not only that the young man was impeded physically but also that he would 'see the situation in a one-eyed way', becoming less able to resist the Bunyip's power. However, he summoned his courage and hurled another spear, with success this time, blinding the Bunyip in one eye and balancing his own disability.

Howling with pain, the Bunyip turned and ran. But the girl was still trapped by his spell, and as the hunter sprang forward to clasp her in his arms, she fled with her savage captor.

The hunter tracked them through the swamp. He followed them over sand flats and into the eucalyptus woodlands near Mount Goombaronga. There the Bunyip climbed an enormous tree, calling the girl to follow. But although she tried to obey his command, she kept sliding back, and finally stood with her back to the trunk, torn between delight at the prospect of rescue and fear of the magic that was drawing her after the Bunyip.

Looking up to see where his enemy was, the hunter froze where he stood, transfixed by the Bunyip's hypnotic stare.

Time stood still for the three actors in the drama. Like the court in *Sleeping Beauty* they were shrouded in sleep: the Bunyip in his tree, the hunter and the girl on the ground. Then one day a violent storm erupted, and with a flash of lightning and a mighty gust of wind the great tree came crashing down. The young people clasped each other in wonder and peered into the wreckage of leaves. There among the branches lay the Bunyip. He had died of his wounds, but that single eye continued to gaze balefully down—it had become the Moon.

The lovers married and lived together for many years, but they had been marked by the experience. The hunter was still blind in one eye. Their children belonged to the frog totem, with the frog as their sacred animal. And when they looked at the night sky they would see the undying eye of the Bunyip watching every move they made.

The Moon is more than a deity of storms and fertility in nature, it is also concerned with the storms and creativity of our inner world. *Lunacy* and *lunatic* come from the Latin word for the Moon. The realm of instinct and the unconscious is a lunar world: its uncertain light reveals shapes of the mind that would otherwise lie hidden, and it was with good reason that the poet Pindar, in Ancient Greece (fifth century BC), records how Aphrodite, 'the bright Moon', taught Jason, the hero who led the Argonauts in search of the Golden Fleece, 'to bring down the dark moon' when he needed the aid of magical powers.

Mrs K. Langloh Parker was an early collector of myths, who, as a child, had been saved from drowning by Aborigines. Many of the stories she wrote down were told to her during that time, when she lived on her father's property on the Darling River, with mainly Aboriginal children as playmates.

One sequence she recorded concerns Bahloo the Moon, charting his development from mortal, to Moon-Man, to Moon Deity.

In his human form, Bahloo was called Nullandi, the happy man. He was fond of his wives and family, and a great contrast to his friend Loolo, the sad man. Nullandi kept his family well supplied with food, played with his children, taught them well and did everything an ideal husband and father should do. So far there is no hint of the strange destiny that lay in store for him.

Whereas Nullandi saw everything for the best in the best of all possible worlds, Loolo was a pessimist whose doleful complaints about the lack of game and the ingratitude of wives and children were constantly fulfilled. 'There are fewer kangaroos than there used to be,' he would complain ill-naturedly, although Nullandi seemed to find all he needed to support *his* family. Loolo was deeply afraid of old age and death. 'When we die, that's the end of us,' he said, as he walked home with Nullandi one day. 'The life we have here isn't worth living, and there's nothing after death to look forward to. Our time ends, and we don't come back.'

'Well, it won't be like that for me,' said Nullandi, unconvinced, and already making the sort of assured prediction we hear from prospective Moon-Men. 'I like life and my family too much.' He pointed to the east: 'I'll become the Moon. I may have a short death each month, but I'll have to put up with that, and I'll soon return, shining away as before.'

'Don't deceive yourself,' snapped Loolo, 'you're as mortal as the rest of us. When your spirit leaves your body that will be the finish.'

Nullandi was angered at last. 'We'll both return,' he said. 'I'll be the Moon, and you'll be a blue fish in the sea—good enough for you too.'

That was the end of their friendship, but when they died Baiame, the All-Father, the great Sky-God of southeast Australia, made Nullandi's prediction come true. He did become the Moon-Man under the name of Bahloo, and Loolo returned as a blue fish.

When Nullandi spoke of coming back as the Moon, his mortal imagination couldn't grasp what the change would mean. Reincarnated as Bahloo the Moon-Man, he became a being very different from the carefree individual of the past.

We meet him next living uneasily in the sky. Yhi, the Sun-Woman, had many lovers. She was a hot-blooded passionate creature and soon turned her amorous attention to Bahloo, pressuring him incessantly to become her lover. She pursued him across the sky and even ordered the spirits who held each corner like a blue blanket, to drive him back. But Bahloo assumed the shape of an emu, slipped by the unsuspecting sky-guardians and descended to earth to revisit his wives.

In his absence those women had become frustrated and were sleeping with his three brothers. It didn't take Bahloo long to realise what was happening, especially when the youngest wife awoke and sleepily called him by the wrong name. Nor did it take greatly enhanced powers to guess that the brothers would soon attack him and try to keep the women for themselves.

Bahloo was swift to make a plan. He took the log of a minggah, or spirit-animated tree, laid it beside his wives, and covered it with a kangaroo skin to look like his own sleeping form. Then he hid in the shadows and waited. In the middle of the night his brothers crept into the gunyah and stood looking down at the bundle he had made. 'That must be Bahloo,' they whispered, 'let's finish him once and for all.' Raising their nulla-nullas they pounded the bundle so fiercely that nothing within it could have survived; then, well pleased with their work, they hurried off into the night. The minggah, which could move invisibly of its own accord, disappeared, and Bahloo took its place under the kangaroo skin as if nothing had happened.

But although he had tricked his brothers, the incident showed that he no longer had a place in the normal affairs of his family. He was the Moon, and the Moon is husband to all women. So Bahloo became the creator of girl babies. In this he was assisted by Wahn the crow. But Wahn was a bad-tempered bird, and his babies grew up to be shrewish ill-natured women with loud voices and jealous dispositions. Men thought that in spite of Bahloo's romantic proclivities it was better to have him making the babies than Wahn. When the Moon rose late, they would say: 'Bahloo must have made a lot of babies tonight.' They would smile in envy, and instructing their daughters not to catch his attention, they would glance at their pregnant wives and breathe a sigh of relief.

One myth has Wahn and Bahloo arguing as to whether men and women should be reborn, and Wahn trapping Bahloo in the sky by the familiar trick of the rising tree. But this seems a tributary to the mainstream of Bahloo's story.

There was more than a little affection for Bahloo. When the winter Moon looked yellow after it had risen, people would say: 'Bahloo knows there will be a frost. He is keeping warm tonight—see how brightly his camp-fire glows!' When there was a halo round the moon, they would say: 'Bahloo has built his *dardurr* [a shelter made of bark] —it will rain!'

These stories are good-humoured and make us feel that Bahloo still retains much of his mortal nature: practical joker, protector of women, maker of cheerful girls. But two subsequent myths show him in quite a different light. In these the transformation is complete. The easy-going Bahloo has become a Moon-God, dangerous, possessed of strange powers, and not hesitant to use them.

Mooregoo the mopoke lived alone and occupied himself by making weapons and possum-skin rugs. He carved his boomerangs with the teeth of possums, and sewed his rugs with possum sinews threaded on a needle made with a small bone from the leg of an emu. Proud of his work, he kept the weapons and rugs for himself and gave none away.

Bahloo the Moon heard of this and one night came peering in Mooregoo's door to see for himself. 'Very nice,' he murmured, when he had examined the work. Then he made the first of four calculated requests. 'Lend me one of your possum-skin rugs, Mooregoo.'

'I do not lend my rugs,' said Mooregoo sharply.

'Then give me one.'

'I do not give my rugs,' came the irritated reply.

Bahloo frowned and looked at the finely carved boomerangs, and spears, and nullah-nullahs. 'Give me some of your weapons?' he urged.

'I never give the weapons I have made to anyone else,' snapped Mooregoo.

Bahloo's frown deepened as he made his last request. 'It's a frosty night and very cold,' he said. 'Please lend me one of your rugs.'

But Mooregoo shook his head stubbornly. 'You should listen more carefully,' he said. 'I told you once and I'll tell you again: I do not lend my rugs or my weapons. I don't lend them and I don't give them away.'

'Very well,' said Bahloo and left him.

As well as the obligation of hospitality, Mooregoo had a special obligation to

Bahloo, for the materials he had used came from Moon animals and Bahloo had a claim on the results. He had asked four ritual questions, and when they were refused, he became entitled to the revenge that swiftly followed.

Bahloo retreated to the hills, where he cut some bark and made himself a *dardurr*. Then he stood in front of it, raised his arms to the sky, and called down the rains. Safe inside his shelter on high ground, he lay quietly and listened to the rain pouring down. Day after day it fell, until the countryside below was flooded. Mooregoo was drowned, his rugs rotted, and the weapons he had prized so much floated away.

By nature the Moon is a law-giver; he makes rules and enforces them. Mooregoo had four opportunities to obey. He refused them all, and perished in the floods which the Moon has always at his command.

Another myth about Bahloo returns to the argument he had with Loolo, and follows the tradition of a chance for eternal life offered by the Moon, but rejected.

Bahloo came down to the earth one night with his three hunting companions. It should not surprise us to learn that they were snakes—a black snake, a tiger snake, and a death adder—for the snake shares a triple power with the Moon: self-renewal, knowledge of the underworld, and a phallic nature.

During the hunt Bahloo came to a river beside whose swiftly-flowing waters stood a group of Aborigines. He greeted them with a request: 'I want you to pick up my snakes and carry them to the other side of the river,' he said.

The men were terrified. 'We honour you, Bahloo,' they whispered unhappily, 'but we're afraid of your snakes. If we pick them up, they'll bite us, and we'll die.'

'If you honour me, do as I say,' said Bahloo. And we can imagine the scene as he speaks: moonlight trees, writhing snakes, shadowy figures gathered by the shore of the dark river. Taking a piece of bark, he tossed it into the swiftly flowing stream. 'Listen,' he went on. 'If you carry my snakes to the other side, you'll be like that piece of bark. When it falls in the water it goes under for a moment, but, see, it rises again and floats on. That's how it is with me, and that's how it will be with you if you do as I tell you. Take my snakes to the other side, and when you die you will always come to life again.'

The Aborigines listened but they were still too frightened to do as he asked.

Bahloo picked up a large black stone. 'Listen again,' he said ominously, as he tossed it into the river. 'Hear the dead sound it makes when it hits the water. A stone does not rise like a piece of bark. It lies in darkness at the bottom and is never seen again.'

The men knew what he was telling them. They looked at Bahloo, and down at his hissing snakes. 'We can't do it,' they muttered. 'We are too afraid.'

'As you wish,' said Bahloo, 'I'll carry them over myself.' He coiled the black snake around one arm, the tiger snake around the other, and set the death adder on his shoulder. Then he swam the angry river and stood on the other side looking back at the men. After a long moment, he picked up another stone and tossed it high in the air. The men watched as it seemed to rise and rise in slow motion, falling with a splash that filled the moonlight with spray. 'That is the sound of your death,' said Bahloo. 'You could have lived many lives, but the moment has passed. When you die, you'll become a part of the earth and lie in the dark like that stone.'

The myth has great imaginative power, and it is interesting to see how similar it is to the myths of death, and revival foregone, from Arnhem Land and Melville Island, at the northern end of the continent.

The First Death

In many cases, the older the myth, the more important the animal form becomes.[24] There is a process of transition from the Moon Deity as an animal, to the spirit of the Deity as an animal, and finally to a situation where the Deity is merely attended by the animal. Hecate, for example was once a hound with three heads, Artemis a bear, and Cybele a lion. Later, in more sophisticated times, these creatures split from the person of the Goddess and dwindled to form part of her entourage.

The fish is a creature with strong Christian associations. The Age of Pisces was the great age of Christianity. Both Christian and Gnostic texts refer to Christ as Ichthyos, the fish, and a medieval hymn calls Him 'the little fish that the Virgin caught in her fountain'.[25]

In Aboriginal lore, one of the few myths to depict the Moon in non-human form (as opposed to an object like a bone or a boomerang) shows it as a fish.[26]

During the Dreamtime two sisters called Nakari and Kurramara travelled to Bribie Island, off the Sunshine Coast of Queensland, looking for food. Nakari carried a baby on her shoulders, but in spite of that they were self-sufficient girls and could look after themselves.

They wandered fearlessly across the island and found a saltwater lagoon, where they made camp and built a *mia-mia* for shelter. There were plenty of yams and shellfish, and the lagoon was so well stocked with fish that there seemed no need to go anywhere else.

They were carefree and full of high spirits, and the first morning they caught a fish the like of which they had never seen before: large, round, and glowing with a silvery inner light. Back in camp they built a fire, buried the fish in the hot ash beneath the coals, and, because such a big fish would take time to cook, they walked into the bush to dig up yams as a garnish to go with it.

When they returned, the ashes were mysteriously scattered, and the wonderful fish was gone. Speculating on what could have happened, the two sisters followed the trail of ash until they reached a tall bloodwood tree. There, among the branches, they saw the fish, still glowing faintly and pulling itself steadily up the trunk.

'I'll watch the fish,' said Kurramara, the elder sister, to Nakari. 'You run back to the camp and bring our spears and sticks.'

While Nakari sped off, Kurramurra did everything she could to dislodge the fish, throwing stones at it and shaking the tree, but without success, and by the time Nakari returned the fish had climbed too high to reach.

'Maybe the top branches will give way and it will fall down,' said Kurramara hopefully—but that didn't happen. Instead, the fish suddenly launched itself into the sky and the sisters stood watching it move slowly westward like a dim light.

They were very dissatisfied with that. Although they had witnessed a remarkable happening, they had also been robbed of a good meal, and that was really what mattered.

Next morning they took the baby and walked to the beach. Nakari laid the child on the sand and covered it with a possum-skin rug while she and her sister went looking for shellfish. There were plenty to be found, and the girls were so occupied with what they were doing that they failed to notice the tide coming in. When they did, it was too late: the waves had buried the child in the sand until only a foot was showing.

Let us pause here and consider what has happened so far. The two girls had a special rapport with the Moon; they had taken it from the sea in its fish form and somehow provided the opportunity for it to find its natural place in the sky.

This was the birth of the Moon from the sea, and the two sisters, in spite of not really understanding what had taken place, had presided over the change. They were gathering shellfish, which belong to the Moon, while the child, wrapped in a possum-skin rug, had been drowned by the tide, whose ebb and flow is also governed by the Moon. The child had been surrounded by Moon influences, and in myth such a death must be regarded as intended by the Moon, not as a random event.

Sadly the sisters buried the child, and walked hand-in-hand along the beach. After swimming the channel to the mainland, they spent the night in a cave near Caloundra, and next morning followed the beach to Mooloolah Heads, where they swam another passage to Maroochy Beach. It was almost as if they had been led there. As they stood on the edge of the beach, with waves breaking over their feet, a huge log suddenly appeared on the surface of the sea, forming a bridge from the beach to an island called Mudjimba. Without hesitation the girls crossed the log, and as they stepped ashore, it vanished, stranding them on Mudjimba.

'I hope you like this place, sister,' said Kurramara. 'It's too far to swim back.'

'We'll live here forever then,' said Nakari, who was still grieving for the dead child. 'There are breadfruit and yams ...'

'And crabs, and shellfish, and fish,' finished Kurramara. 'Don't worry. We'll manage.'

Although they were worn out with all that had happened, they had enough strength to make a fire. The wood caught at once, but the smoke behaved in a strange way. Instead of swirling or blowing over them, it rose straight up into the calm air like a phantom rope linking them to the sky.

Darkness settled on the island, and the two sisters were dozing by their fire when the Moon rose slowly out of the sea. 'Look,' cried Nakari, 'there's that fish we caught.'

'It certainly was a big one,' said Kurramara.

'The biggest fish in the world,' said Nakari softly, 'and we caught it.'

They watched the Moon all night, uncertain whether they were dreaming or awake. Each night they watched it grow smaller as if it was being eaten, until there was nothing left. 'It's all gone,' said Nakari. Like my baby, she thought.

The girls sat on by the fire, and after three days a slim crescent of their fish appeared once more. 'Our fish has come back,' said Nakari.

'I think it will always come back,' said her sister, 'and we'll be here to see it.'

Soon they did not move again, and the smoke seemed to hold them there like a rope in the sky. They had become Moon-Women. The Moon had given them a destiny into which Nakari's child did not fit. A child, of its nature, means growth and change, so the Moon, which does not tolerate competition in the lives of its priestesses, took this inconvenient child to the land of the dead, over which it presides in its three dark days.

Moon enchantment provided the sisters with access to a sacred island, holding them there with its rope of smoke and hypnotic splendour until the end of the Dreamtime when they entered the landscape. It may also be that they were involved in a process of humanising its animal nature. Of course, traditional people do not design their myths in this self-conscious analytical way. They establish a set of deeply-felt images, and the stories tell themselves.

As fish are very lively on moonlit nights, there is a practical reason for associating them with the Moon. We know too that the fish as a symbol combines a broad range of meanings with lunar associations: its origin in the sea, its remarkable fertility through the number of its eggs, which made it a symbol of fecundity among peoples as diverse as the Babylonians, the Phoenicians, the Assyrians and the Chinese, and as an image of instinct and the unconscious. However, meaning lies not in amplifying comments, fascinating as these may be, but in the poetry and resonance of images that still entrance us—like the age-old presence of two sisters who sit by an enchanted fire and follow the changes of the Moon that was once a fish they caught in a nearby lagoon.

☾ ☾ ☾

In common with other myths, those concerning the Moon exist on many different levels of purpose and imagination. You cannot make a more basic statement than to tell a child that the new Moon is a boomerang tossed in the sky; nor a more cautionary one than the myth of *The Man in the Moon*, about a surly peasant banished from earth for working on Sunday.

Still simple, but more engaging, are the stories that explain how the natural world came to be as it is, why crows are black, for example; and in the case of *The Arm of Tukutita*, why dingoes bay at the moon.

In *The Arm of Tukutita* we learn that Tutratta, a giant dingo, had preyed on members of the Aluridja tribe for as long as people could remember. When he was hungry he simply seized the first person to cross his path and tore him to pieces.

One day, Tukutita, the fleetest runner in the tribe, was out hunting kangaroos (whose great leaps he had learned to imitate), when he met Tutratta on the prowl. The nightmare creature gave chase, but Tukutita sprang into the sky and sprinted to safety along the ridge of a bank of clouds.

Tutratta was foiled for the present, but he knew that hunger would drive his intended victim back to earth, and he was prepared to wait. Soon Tukutita did grow hungry. He leapt from the clouds to a tree and began to feed on the possums playing there. As well as being fleet of foot, he was a greedy man and gorged himself on so much possum meat that he grew lazy, and instead of remaining on guard he slid to the ground and sauntered back to camp as if nothing could harm him.

This was Tutratta's chance. With a snarl of triumph he resumed the chase, and this time Tukutita's famous turn of speed was slowed by the food he had eaten. Tutratta caught him easily, dragged him to the ground and ate him up, except for an arm bone, which flew like a boomerang into the sky—there to become the crescent Moon. Tutratta lifted his head in a howl of disappointment, but there was nothing he could do to get it back. Since then, all dingoes howl like Tutratta when they see the Moon. They want that arm bone too.

Some myths, less picturesque to the average reader, are important social statements and present the Moon as a legislator of tribal law.

The Aboriginal kinship rules governing marriage are among the most complex in the world, and a Moon myth reported by Spencer and Gillen in *Native Tribes of Central Australia* provides a blueprint of how they work. In this tradition the Moon first appeared in the form of a Purula man named Pulla, who came from the sea to a place named Kulla Kulla, where many women lived. From among these he stole a woman who stood in the relationship of father's sister's daughter to him. This meant that under the tribal laws of marriage he could not take her as his proper wife, but that did not deter Pulla, and although the other women tried to prevent the abduction, he was too strong for them.

Next he went on to Uningamara, where he took a Panunga woman, whom he left as soon as she bore him a child. Then he turned his attention to a Kumara woman, pretending he was an Appungati man, which would have been an approved relationship. He left the Kumara woman as soon as she had a child, and went on to a woman of the Thungalla, treating her the same way. One after another he took women from six tribes, abandoning each when she had a child. For some time he settled in a place called Ariltha-unina where he had many wives, and after all this experience he began to instruct the men of the tribes concerning the proper wives for each class of man to take.

This is the main thrust of the myth: a justification of the strict taboos surrounding marriage by presenting them as a system handed down by the Moon, husband of all women, during the Dreamtime.

In his old age Pulla settled once more in Kulla Kulla, where an old man came to his camp to steal a woman. The angry Moon-Man killed him with a stone axe and then rose into the sky, where he can still be seen standing in the Moon with his axe raised—an image contrasting with the Western *Man in the Moon*, who carries a bundle of faggots on his back as an eternal reminder of what happens to those who break the Sabbath.

'Sabbath' is a word and concept inherited from the Babylonians. At full Moon the Goddess Ishtar was said to be menstruating, and because the Moon neither increased or decreased at this time, it was considered a day of 'heart's rest', inappropriate for cooking food or doing other work. Later this *shabbatu*, day of rest, was honoured four times each lunar month—a custom adopted by the Jews and, in due course, by the Christian Church.

It is interesting to note the role of the Moon in the story of the Ten Commandments engraved by God on the Tablets of the Law and given to Moses on Mount Sinai. Moses and Aaron were both Levites, with a tradition of Moon service as well as dedication to the Old Testament God, Yahweh, and as an outward sign of their allegiance may well have worn a headdress with a lunar crescent on it. The name Sinai is derived from Sinn the Babylonian Moon-God (father of the Goddess Ishtar), and Mount Sinai, sacred to him, is therefore a Moon Mountain. Sinn had been a law-giver long before the period ascribed to Moses, who as a Levite would have seen it as a very appropriate place to seek and find the rules to govern the conduct of his people.[27] It should be noted that we do not know for certain whether Moses is an historical leader or a mythic hero, nor do we know which of a number of candidates is the mountain referred to; Jebel Musa (Mountain of Moses), in the southern part of the Sinai Peninsula, is a favourite choice of modern scholars.[28]

Such glimpses of the Moon as law-giver and the source of many traditions we no longer associate with it are a reminder of the complex social issues that some myths can raise—a dimension easy to overlook in the versions we habitually see.

The First Dawn

It will be recalled that in the Aboriginal tradition humanity did not fall from grace. There was no loss of innocence or expulsion from Paradise. The Dreamtime remained immanent, always available when a channel of entry was opened through the right ceremony.

However, there is a theme that the myths of the Dreamtime share with the Garden of Eden, and that is the creation of woman from the body of man. In the early Dreamtime, as in early Eden, woman did not exist, and the myth of *Moon and Morning Star* tells how this was accomplished by the Moon.[29]

During the northwest monsoon, the sand-beach people shelter in round tea-tree huts in the bush, waiting for the end of the rains and the start of the dry season. Then they return to the beach and camp by the sea. It is a time of abundance and joy. The tides bring in fish, which the men spear with stingray-barbed spears, and edible shellfish, which the women gather in dilly-bags at low tide. In the minds of the sand-beach people, these good things are always associated with the Moon, which leads the Morning Star from the northeast until they sink together over the western rim of the sea.

This myth concerns two newly initiated young men who came from the northeast and travelled south from what are now the shores of the Gulf of Carpentaria. They had no wives, for although the need for feminine companionship was powerfully felt, there were no women in the world. As they wrestled and danced their way along, the young men sang the song *Te-tyámpa*:

I go up into the scrub
To make a club
You cook meanwhile!
I go up into the scrub
You be cooking the while!
Now in the moonlight
Let's dance and sing.

As they romped along, they created both sea and landscape. Moon, the elder brother, made a stingray-barbed spear and speared fish and stingrays with it. This was the springtime of the world, and the hearts of both brothers were light as they shouted their song, laid down their spears to wrestle and dance, and then picked them up again for more fishing.

'You cook the stingray, while I sing,' said Moon, and Morning Star was happy to do that. 'Here's yours, here's mine,' he said, dividing up the meal.

The rhythm of the song pervades the tale: how the younger brother kindled the fire, gathered bark and prepared the fish ... how the elder brother sat singing and clapping his hands, and told his companion to bring the food to him.

At night they lit two fires: 'Lay yours to the south, and mine to the north,' said the elder brother. They lay between them in the light of the full Moon and after a brief rest began singing and clapping their hands again.

So it goes on, the elder brother spearing stingray and catfish, mullet and kingfish, the younger brother cooking them and fetching water from the wells in a bailer shell.

At Yo'inka they made a river and camped on its bank. Before they arrived, the sea did not exist, only a small creek meandering along the sand-beach with a vista of endless scrub stretching away to the west. There was insufficient room for the teeming abundance of creation, so Moon threw a boomerang westwards. It curved through the bright air in a great circle, felling the scrub and returning once more. Again and again the scything boomerang cut through the scrub, and as the brothers moved westward the sea followed them, inundating the cleared land.

They formed sandbanks, and as they waded out into the sea the tide ebbed around them. When they returned it followed them in, and they went on felling scrub with their moon-shaped boomerangs until at last it was time to rest. They made their fires, ate, and wrestled, and sang, until the elder brother said: 'Let's sleep now.' He had no woman to console him, but he had devised a plan. I'll use my brother for that, he thought.

While Morning Star slept, Moon took his boomerang and began to carve and mould the boy's body. His brother felt nothing. His sleep was as deep as the sleep of Adam when Eve was created from one of his ribs.

When Morning Star awoke he looked down at himself and cried: 'What has happened to me in the night? I was a man then, but I've changed completely.'

Moon merely said: 'You are no longer my brother, you are my wife.'

He picked up Morning Star's spears and put them with his own. They stayed three days where they were, for all this happened in the mysterious dark of the Moon. The husband shaped a yamstick for his wife. She made a dilly-bag from the fibre of the wild fig tree and used it in gathering shellfish. She also made a large basket in which to carry the yams she unearthed with her stick, and so the separate duties of men and women were established.

The couple continued as before, the husband throwing his boomerang, the wife cooking and laying the fires, the tide ebbing as they walked out from the shore and rising as they returned. At night they would lie side by side, the husband singing his song, the wife listening to his voice in the soft night.

At last their journey came to an end in a place called Pinmanka. There they camped, and there they remained as husband and wife forever.

Moon and Morning Star had shaped the countryside, made the sea, set the ebb and flow of the tides, and established the separate duties of men and women. Their journey across the Gulf reflects the setting of the Moon and the Morning Star in the west; their path is the silver track of the Moon on the Gulf water. Moon had made the first woman, and to record it all they left behind them the song *Te-tyámpa*, which has been sung by the sand-beach people ever since.

For the inland Wikmunkan, however, the Moon is associated not with the sea and its tides but with water holes and swamps. The name of the Moon

Hero is Kappa. He was the first to catch fish by stupefying them with poisonous plants. The men from across the river were so jealous of the quantity of fish Kappa speared that one of them, Tye-li the swamp-fish, speared him in revenge. But before Kappa died, he speared Tye-li too and they both disappeared into the water. Kappa can be seen there today as a reflection of the Moon; and with the help of poison plants, men continue to make good catches of swamp-fish as Kappa showed them.[30]

The scene of *The Death of Gidja*, the last Aboriginal myth in this collection, is a waterfall of the Roaring Meg, a stream that rises in rugged mountain country and flows into the Bloomfield River.[31] The deep pools of the Roaring Meg are said to be inhabited by a great eel or serpent called the Yaro, whose appearance is made even more fearsome by a huge head and a mane of red hair.[32] Here, at floodtime, the torrent rages over rapids and waterfalls as it hurls itself westward to join the Bloomfield River on its journey through flat forest country to the Pacific Ocean, between Cooktown and Cape Tribulation on the Queensland coast.

This myth also begins with the creation of woman from the body of a man, but it is more complex, darkly coloured and dramatic than *Moon and Morning Star*.

Gidja the Moon was a man of the Koko-Yalunya tribe. As yet there were no women in the world and, as a result, no children either.

Yalungur the eaglehawk was a handsome young man. He had long, soft hair, a slim body and a generally feminine appearance. Watching him bathe in the stream one day, Gidja decided to make him into a wife, in spite of the fact that they both belonged to the *Dabu* moiety. Moiety is a word meaning half—in this case, half of a tribe. The other half of the Koko-Yalunya was called *Wallar*, and social contact between the two groups was strictly limited.

Waiting until Yalungur had fallen asleep, Gidja took a knife of white stone and began to operate, carving and moulding the body of the young man into that of a woman. When Yalungur awoke he showed no resentment at what had been done, meekly accepting the sex change, and beginning a new life as Gidja's wife.

Next, Gidja wanted a son. He took bark from the bloodwood and milk-wood trees, crushed them and extracted the red and white sap. This he thrust into Yalungur, the blood staying where he had put it, the milk making her breasts swell.

Now he had to mould the unborn child. To do this he picked the crimson flowers of the bottle brush that grows in river beds, and the scarlet flowers of the flame tree that grows in the scrub, enclosing them in a string dilly-bag and mixing them with long-shaped and round-shaped yams. This package he also pushed inside Yalungur and waited—in vain, for the passage was dry and no child emerged. To solve the new problem Gidja used another type of yam, which was good for lubrication. He had begun at sunrise, and by sunset the child was born. 'Gidja made it in one day,' old Wulbur, the narrator of the myth, remarked. 'No one else can do that, and without him we would have no women or children.'

When the tribe heard the child crying, everyone sat up and listened. 'What's that crying?' they asked.

'My son,' replied Gidja proudly. 'He's just been born, and here is the wife I made for myself too.'

Now people began to notice that Yalungur was missing, and finally Gidja was forced to confess what he had done.

Interest turned to outrage. 'You should not have spoiled the boy,' cried one. And another: 'How cruel of you to cut him like that.' Angrily the tribe began to discuss revenge and would have speared Gidja there and then, had they not been afraid of him.

Nugumbi the rat decided to act. With a curved emu bone (a Moon implement with power over life and death) he captured the child's shadow and shut it in the hollow of the bone. Robbed of his shadow, the child grew ill and died. Heartbroken, Gidja made a bark coffin for the little body.

Torrential rain flowed from the grief of the Moon. The falls thundered down the rock face, and storm clouds swept so low they seemed to brush the

tops of the trees. To escape the danger of the low ground where they lived, the tribe decided to cross to the other side of the river by way of a lawyer-vine bridge. Gidja, burdened with the coffin of his dead son, was last on the bridge. When he reached the centre, Kallin-Kallin the chickenhawk, who had his eye on Yalungur for himself, gave a loud shout and slashed the supporting vines. Gidja plunged into the rapids and over the edge of the falls. The coffin caught in a tree, and became a rock which can be seen to this day as proof that the story is true.

Now the men of the tribe began to chase Gidja down the river, spearing him as they went. When he dived out of sight, they waited until he came up and speared him again. Relentless in their pursuit, they followed him to a place called Kalabro and speared him there. He tried to scramble to the bank, but a blow from a stick caught him across the shoulders and knocked him back into the water. His enemies dragged him out thinking that he was dead, but he sprang up shouting: '*Ough! Ah! Ngaiyu Käri Wulan!*—I'm not dead!'

They chased him down the Bloomfield River giving him up for dead again at Amojir. But again he sprang up with the same shout '*Ough! Ah! Ngaiyu Käri Wulan!*'

Determined that he should not escape, they continued the pursuit and finally caught him at Kauwai, where the river flows into the sea. There Gidja

was so badly speared he could go no further. They pulled him out of the water and left him lying on the sand, but when they returned he was nowhere to be seen—a rock stood where his body had lain.

Gidja's spirit took from the body of the blue-tongued lizard a bone shaped like a boomerang and flung it far out to sea. In these days of special effects it is easy to imagine the bone hissing through the air, burning with a cold white flame as it spins, becoming more moonlike, and finally coming to rest in the sky.

Kauwai became a site sacred to the Moon, and a reflection of the rock that marks the place of Gidja's death may be seen as a shadow on its glowing disk.

It is Yalungur, the woman shaped by the Moon, and now grown old, who sends the spirits of unborn babies to the wombs of the mothers who are to give them a new life. She sits on a rock in the mountains, singing softly to herself as she makes her dilly-bags the way Moon did in the old days. The unborn children are called *mulgal-mulgal*, and there are many mysteries connected with their arrival. Sometimes Yalungur will send a snake to find the mother—a woman may start and cry out on finding a snake in her blanket, but one moment it is there and the next it has disappeared. Sometimes the *mulgal-mulgal* appear as butterflies fluttering in the wind and searching for a mother. Sometimes an empty canoe may come floating down the river, sent by the *mulgal-mulgal* as a signal that one of them will soon be born.

The spearings of Gidja, his deaths and resurrections, his cries 'I am not dead!', symbolise the phases of the Moon and its eternal cycle of death and renewal. But the question remains: why did the tribe attack him so fiercely? Gidja was the benefactor of his people—he created the first woman, and his experiments made childbirth possible—yet he was tracked down and killed like a common criminal. This is typical of the problems we face with many Aboriginal myths. Judged from a Western standpoint they may seem fickle, illogical, and even cruel.[33] Yet they command not only a degree of reverence that demands respect, they reward closer examination with profound insights into an immensely complex society, and brilliantly illuminate those mysterious depths of the psyche, common to all, where myths are born.

In this instance, outrage for what Gidja did to Yalungur might be a superficial explanation for the event, but a more powerful reason concerns tribal law. The natural division of Koko-Yalunya society, before the introduction of marriage, was between *Dabu*, the scrub-dwellers, and *Wallar*, who lived in the forest. Gidja was killed because he took a scrub-dweller like himself for a wife, and even his child was doomed because of that. His departure to the sky, however, set the seal on a new era of social stability.

The subsequent marriage of scrub-dwelling Yalungur to Kallin-Kallin of the forest transformed the natural divisions into two interacting kinship groups, which bore the same names, *Dabu* and *Wallar*, thus reflecting a correct attitude towards the tribal law of exogamy that compelled a man to marry outside his own group.

The Death of Gidja, with its geographic, social and totemic subtleties, calls to mind a remark by T.G.H. Strehlow concerning the myths of the Northern Aranda: 'One feels that one is being led into a wide-spread maze, into a vast labyrinth with countless corridors, and passages, and sidewalks, all of which are connected with one another in ramifications that at times appear altogether baffling in their complexity and interdependence.'[34]

Many myths lead to this labyrinth. The reader need not enter it to enjoy the colour and fascination of the stories they tell, but the experience gains depth when a few steps are ventured.

☾ ☾ ☾

In his far-ranging study *The Masks of God*, Joseph Campbell has listed four essential functions of mythology.[35] The first two are to support a sense of awe at the mystery of being and to present an image of the universe that endorses the mystery. The third is social and suggests that mythology strengthens society and helps to integrate its members with their community. The fourth moves to the level of the individual, where myths are a guide to spiritual enrichment and self-realisation.

In this way a living mythology provides traditional people with an atlas of cosmic, social and psychological maps with whose aid they can negotiate the complexities of the universe, their society and their own nature.[36] But traditional people are not alone in needing the sense of meaning these wonderful tales produce. We need it, too, and because the longing is such a profound part of us, the process of myth-creation is never ending.

Most lives contain events that transport us to a mythical dimension and remain writ large in our personal history. The first landing on the Moon was one of these. It did not matter that science produced the miracle. The journey through space, the heroism of the three astronauts, the wonder of possessing a magic mirror that could show the event as it happened, stirred the imagination of millions and demonstrated Campbell's four principles as convincingly as a tribal ceremony.

To show the creation of a modern Moon myth at work, I will describe my own experience.

It is Sunday night, 20 July 1969. I am living in a large block of red-brick apartments near the edge of Holland Park in London. The black and white TV set is on, and into the darkening London evening comes the voice of Buzz Aldrin from the *Eagle* module of *Apollo 11*: 'Throttle full thrust. Breaking hard. Height above the Moon 46,500 feet. Passing near Crater Maskeyline. Touchdown in 10 minutes and 14 seconds...'

The sound of a jet bound for Heathrow whines overhead, but our thoughts are spanning vaster distances than that. We are entering the dimension of myth.

Aldrin's voice continues: '2,700 miles per hour. This is the closest man has ever been to the Moon...' The screen flickers between shots of the control room in Houston, Texas, and the disk of the Moon. 'You're still looking good,' comes from Houston.

It is seven minutes to touchdown. The astronauts are locking into the landing site in the Sea of Tranquillity. 'Good radar data,' comes Neil Armstrong's voice. 'Height now 33,000 feet.'

They are nearing the High Gate, and the small white numbers are racing towards zero. Between beeps, the voices drone figures. 'Velocity now down to 1,200 feet per second. Braking hard...' I'm recording it all in the diary on my knee. The subdued emotion of the voices, the power of the science we have forged, the heroic adventure of man against the universe, the magic and mystery of the Moon itself, provide an overwhelming flood of images. We pan to the crowds in Trafalgar Square for a communal moment, then back to the Moon. The landing site is in view. All the training, all the technique, all the technology will come together in the next few minutes, for better or worse.

The engine of a car guns in the street below. I take a nervous sip of my drink. 'Altitude 4,200 feet,' says Houston control. 'You're go for landing. Over!' 'Hang tight,' comes from Aldrin, 'we're go ...'

Only 2,000 feet now.. 'A new age begins tonight.' I write the words and believe them.

Static. The voices blur. They're nearing the Low Gate, portal to the landing site, a space 8 miles by 4. Armstrong is taking manual control. 'Lights on. 60 seconds. Forward. Good. 40 feet ... Picking up some dust ... Drifting right. Contact light ... OK. Engine stop.' And then the first words from the Moon: 'Houston, Tranquillity Base here. The *Eagle* has landed.' 'Roger, Tranquillity.' Voices relieved, delighted. 'You got a bunch of guys about to turn blue. We're breathing again. Thanks a lot.'

'Landing looks successful,' flashes the caption on the screen. My wife and I hug each other with delight. 'They're there,' she cries. 'It's fantastic.' Here is the strengthening of the social bond. We are a part of the adventure. We are willing the three astronauts to succeed, willing Houston to get it right. In some spine-tingling way, we are contributing to their triumph, which is also our own.

A long pause. Aldrin and Armstrong check the engines, waiting for instructions. And the signal comes: OK to stay on the Moon.

Armstrong begins to describe the scene: 'Football field sized craters. Large numbers of good-sized rocks. Collection of every variety of rock you could find...' Life feels the same, I think, but everything has changed. Nothing will ever be the same again ...

In space, the third astronaut, Mike Collins, is trying to position the lunar bug as he circles the Moon. *Eagle* leans 4½ degrees. That's safe—up to 15 degrees is safe. In a few minutes the crew will close the shutters to cut out the brilliant sunlight. In another minute they will remove their helmets and gloves. No trouble in adjusting to the one-sixth gravity. 'Seems that they landed about four miles from the precise point,' says someone in Houston. 'Pretty good for Government work.'

The wonder of the Moon landing stayed with us throughout the following day. We were happy and excited. Colours were unusually vivid. The commonplace seemed to be touched with a special meaning. Life felt more worthwhile. An Aboriginal would have known at once what had happened to us: we had entered the Dreamtime and returned spiritually refreshed.

The moonwalk took place early next morning. Due at two am, it was six minutes to four when Neil Armstrong stepped onto the surface of the Moon and spoke his famous words.

Fine, black, powdery moondust adhered to the soles of his boots. The crater in which they had landed was indeed about the size of a football field, flat, littered with rocks; a range of hills a mile or so away. Buzz Aldrin joined him. Ghostly, insubstantial, their figures moved through a flickering, white landscape. This really was the Moon. Not a simulation; not a science-fiction story; but our first laboured, lumbering exploration of an alien world. Alien it certainly looked. All I could see was a rubble-strewn wasteland, infinitely inhospitable. And yet, I reminded myself of the oil-rich sheikdoms of the Persian Gulf. What secrets, what unsuspected treasures lay beneath the feet of the two astronauts whose glimmering phantoms moved back and forth, collecting samples, setting up experiments, erecting the memorial plaque: *We men of the planet Earth ... came in peace for all mankind.*

Of course the world didn't change. Greed, inequality, racial prejudice, overpopulation, pressure on the environment, all remained. But the human spirit had been stirred by a great adventure, we were all richer for that, and in the depths of our inner world a new enlivening myth had been born. We had seen three modern shamans soar skywards, two of them to land on the Moon in a vessel named *Eagle*, and return from an unknown world with a healing message—healing for what the old hermits called *accidie*, the boredom and despair of a life that has lost its meaning. It is an interesting coincidence that the eagle was the spirit-form that traditional shamans often adopted to explore the supernatural worlds they visited on healing missions.

Renewal of meaning is the great message of living myth. The self we share with the world may tell us that the Moon is an airless desert of craters and moondust. But in our private world, the realm of hope and dreams, the phantom *wandjina*-like spirits who stepped from the *Eagle* shine on the wall of memory to fertilise the soul;[37] the Garden of the Moons has the richest soil on earth; and the silver mantle of moonlight on the water is the path that Moon and Morning Star trod when they shaped the landscape and gave woman to the world, in that far-off time that is past, present and forever.

Man of Magic

Notes

1 See Mircea Eliade, *Patterns in Comparative Religion.*

2 Phillip Adams, *Weekend Australian*, 26–27 October 1991.

3 Ronald M. Berndt, *Song Cycle of the Moonbone.*

4 Catherine M. Berndt, *Land of the Rainbow Snake.*

5 *Altjirana nambakala*: a phrase quoted in this connection by T.G.H. Strehlow in *Aranda Traditions.*

6 Ronald M. and Catherine H. Berndt, *The Speaking Land*, chapter 1.

7 *Ibid.*

8 Mircea Eliade, *Patterns in Comparative Religion*, p. 155.

9 M. Ester Harding, *Women's Mysteries.*

10 The account used here is based on an unpublished version collected by Charles P. Mountford.

11 M. Esther Harding, *Women's Mysteries.*

12 Robert Graves, *The White Goddess.*

13 This fairytale has been made into an opera called *Der Mond* by Carl Orff (1895–1982), composer of *Carmina Burana*. In a charming addition to the story, St Peter joins the dead in their revels: 'Take the advice of an old man,' he says, 'and enjoy yourselves while you can.'

14 Mircea Eliade, *Patterns in Comparative Religion*, p. 154.

15 My thanks to Mr Stuart Kaye, who discovered in the Launceston Public Library a rare collection of Tasmanian myths by Jackson Cotton, and made them available to Ainslie Roberts and me.

16 Dr Wyatt's essay on the Encounter Bay tribe, in Taplin *et al.*, *Native Tribes of South Australia*, 1879.

17 A comment by S. Gason in his essay on the Dieyerie tribe, in Taplin *et al.*, *Native Tribes of South Australia.*

18 Mircea Eliade, *Patterns in Comparative Religion*, p. 158.

19 T.G.H Strehlow, quoted by Mircea Eliade in *Australian Religions*, p. 57.

20 M. Esther Harding, *Women's Mysteries.*

21 *Ibid.*

22 In *Tiddalik, the Floodmaker*. From *The Dreamtime*, with Ainslie Roberts.

23 C.W. Peck, *Australian Legends.*

24 M. Ester Harding, *Women's Mysteries.*

25 *Ibid.*

26 This myth was collected and poetically retold by Alan Marshall in *The People of the Dreamtime.*

27 M. Ester Harding, *Womens Mysteries.*

28 Robin Lane-Fox, *The Unauthorised Version.*

29 For a detailed account of this myth, see Ursula H. McConnel, *Myths of the Mungkan*. The song *Te-tyámpa* as shown here has been adapted from the translation used in this account.

30 *Ibid.*

31 For a splendid account of this myth and the landscape in which it is set, see Ursula H. McConnel, *A Moon Legend from the Bloomfield River.*

32 Jennifer Isaacs, *Australian Dreaming.*

33 An observation made by James G. Cowan in *Myths of the Dreaming.*

34 T.G.H Strehlow, *Aranda Traditions.*

35 Joseph Campbell, *The Masks of God*, vol. 4, pp. 4–6.

36 Charles E. Hulley, *Ainslie Roberts and the Dreamtime*, p. 107.

37 The mysterious *Wandjina* spirit paintings of the Kimberley Region of Western Australia have no mouths, and the rounded heads faintly resemble an astronaut's protective helmet. Each *Wandjina* is associated with a particular plant or creature. At the end of the creation period the *Wandjinas* painted their likenesses on cave walls and decreed that these should be renewed at the beginning of each wet season. The renewal would give them power to impregnate the species and ensure an abundance of food. I have never seen this combination of rain, fertility and moonlike head-dress directly associated with the Moon, but it is an interesting speculation.

Selected Bibliography

Beier, Ulli (ed.), *Sun and Moon in Papua New Guinea Folklore*, Institute of Papua New Guinea Studies, 1974.

Berndt, Catherine H., *Land of the Rainbow Snake*, John Ferguson, 1981.

Berndt, Ronald M., A Wonguri-Mandjikai song cycle of the Moon-Bone. *Oceania*, 1948a, vol. XIX, no. 1.

Berndt, Ronald M., and Berndt, Catherine H., with John E. Stanton, *Aboriginal Australian Art*, Methuen, 1982.

Berndt, Ronald M., and Berndt, Catherine H., *The World of the First Australians*, Rigby, 1985 edition.

——, *The Speaking Land*, Penguin, 1989.

Campbell, Joseph, *The Hero with a Thousand Faces*, Bolingen series XVII, Princeton University Press, 1968 edition.

——, *The Masks of God*, vol. 1 *Primitive Mythology*, vol. 4 *Creative Mythology*, Viking, 1972.

Charlesworth, M., Morphy, H., Bell, D., and Maddock, K. (eds), *Religion in Aboriginal Australia*, University of Queensland Press, 1984.

Cotton, Jackson, 58-page collection of Tasmanian myths, Launceston Library.

Cowan, James G., *Sacred Places in Australia*, with photographs by Colin Beard, Simon & Schuster, 1991.

——, *Myths of the Dreaming*, Prism Press, 1994.

Donaldson, Ian and Tamsin (eds), *Seeing the First Australians*, Allen & Unwin, 1985.

Eliade, Mircea, *Patterns in Comparative Religion*, Sheed & Ward, 1958.

——, *Australian Religions*, Cornell Press, 1973.

Elkin, A.P., The Secret Life of the Aborigines, *Oceania*, 1932–33, vol. III.

——, *The Australian Aborigines*, Angus & Robertson, 1970 edition.

——, *Aboriginal Men of High Degree*, Queensland University Press, 1977 edition.

Frazer, Sir James, *The Golden Bough*, 3rd edition, Macmillan, 1976, 13 vols.

The Complete Grimm's Fairy Tales, Pantheon Books, 1972 edition, with commentary by Joseph Campbell, and introduction by Padraic Colum.

Graves, Robert, *The White Goddess*, Faber, 1961.

Harding, M. Esther, *Women's Mysteries, Ancient and Modern*, Rider, 1971.

Harney, W.E., *Tales from the Aborigines*, Robert Hale, 1959.

Hernandez, T., Myths and Symbols of the Drysdale River Aborigines, *Oceania*, December 1961, vol. XXXII.

Horton, David (general editor), *The Encyclopaedia of Aboriginal Australia*, Aboriginal Studies Press for the Australian Institute of Aboriginal and Torres Strait Islander Studies, 1994.

Hulley, Charles E., *Ainslie Roberts and the Dreamtime*, J.M. Dent, 1988.

Isaacs, Jennifer (compiler and editor), *Australian Dreaming: 40,000 Years of Aboriginal History*, Lansdowne Press, 1980.

Lane-Fox, Robin, *The Unauthorised Version*, Viking, 1991.

Levy, G.R. *The Gate of Horn*, Faber, 1948.

McConnel, Ursula H., A Moon Legend from the Bloomfield River, North Queensland, *Oceania*, September 1931, vol. 11, no. 1.

——, Myths of the Wilmunkan and Wiknalara Tribes, *Oceania*, 1935b, vol. VI, no. 1.

——, Totemic Hero Cults in Cape York Peninsula, North Queensland, *Oceania*, 1936, vol. VI, no. 1.

——, *Myths of the Mungkan*, Melbourne University Press, 1957.

Marshall, Allan, *The People of the Dreamtime*, F.W. Cheshire, Melbourne, 1952.

Mountford, C.P., *The Moon-Man Wira, and his Revenge*, typed myth 8a, unpublished.

——, *Records of the American-Australian Scientific Expedition to Arnhemland*, vol. 1 *Art, Myths and Symbolism*, Melbourne University Press, 1956.

——, *The Tiwi: Their Art, Myths, and Ceremonies*, Phoenix House, 1958.

——, *Nomads of the Australian Desert*, Rigby, 1976.
——, *Aboriginal Conception Beliefs*, Hyland House, 1981.
Mowaljarlai, David, and Malnic, Jutta, *Yorro Yorro—Everything Standing Up Alive: Spirit of the Kimberley*, Magabala Books, Broome, 1993.
O'Neil, Paul, So Long to the Good Old Moon, *Life*, special edition *To the Moon and Back*, 1969.
Parker, K. Langloh (ed. H. Drake Brockman), *Australian Legendary Tales*, Angus & Robertson, 1953.
Peck, C.W., *Australian Legends*, Stafford & Co., 1925.
Reed, A.W. , *Myths and Legends of Australia*, A.H. & A.W. Reed, 1965.
Roberts, Ainslie (with C.P. Mountford)
——, *The Dreamtime*, Rigby, 1965.
——, *The Dawn of Time*, Rigby, 1969
——, *The First Sunrise*, Rigby, 1971.
——, *The Dreamtime Book*, Rigby, 1973.
(with Melva Jean Roberts):
——, *Dreamtime Heritage*, Rigby, 1975.
——, *Dreamtime: The Aboriginal Heritage*, Rigby, 1981.
(with Dale Roberts):
——, *Echoes of the Dreamtime*, J.M. Dent, 1988.
——, *Shadows in the Mist*, Art Australia, 1989.
Robinson, Roland, *Aboriginal Myths and Legends*, Sun Books, 1966.
Sheldrake, Rupert, *The Rebirth of Nature*, Rider, 1991.
Spencer, B. and Gillen, F.J., *The Arunta*, 2 vols, Macmillan, 1927.
——, *The Native Tribes of Central Australia*, Macmillan, 1938.
Stanner. W.E.H., *White Man Got No Dreaming*, Australian National University Press, 1979.
Strehlow. T.G.H., *Aranda Traditions*, Melbourne University Press, 1947.
Taplin, Rev. George, Wyatt, Dr, Meyer, Rev. A., Schurmann, Rev. C.W. and Gason, S., *Native Tribes of South Australia*, E.S. Wigg & Son, Adelaide, 1879.

Acknowledgements

Known owners of paintings reproduced in this book but not in the possession of Charles E. Hulley or the immediate family of the late Ainslie Roberts are as follows:

S.A. Brewing Company: *Bima the Frightened Curlew.*
Mr and Mrs J. Romanowski: *The First Death.*
Dr D.C. McCarthy: *Rebirth of Japara.*
Mr Ken Mountford: *Sun-Woman and Moon-Man.*
Mrs Bay McDonald: *Numbakulla and the Inapatua.*
Mr Steve Carapetis: *Birthplace of the Moons.*
Mr and Mrs W. Parsons: *The Search for Moodai.*
Fred and Anna Maria Agar: *The Night the Moon Cried.*
Mrs Maughan Thiem: *The Flood Maker.*
Mr and Mrs R. Squire: *Man of Magic.*
Stuart Kaye: *The Melting Moon*, painted by Rhys R. Roberts
from the photograph of a prestudy by Ainslie Roberts.